The

Goldfish

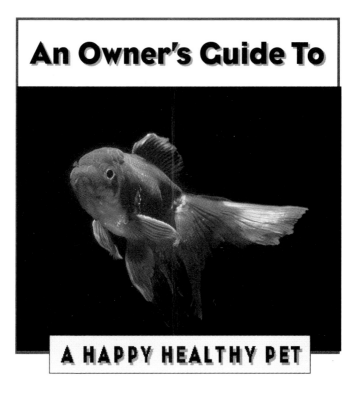

An Owner's Guide To

A HAPPY HEALTHY PET

Howell Book House

Howell Book House
A Simon & Schuster Macmillan Company
1633 Broadway
New York, NY 10019

Library of Congress Cataloging-in-Publication Data
DeVito, Carlo.
The Goldfish: An Owner's Guide to a Happy Healthy Pet/[Carlo DeVito with
Gregory Skomal].
p. cm.
Includes bibliographical references.

ISBN: 0-87605-398-3

1. Goldfish. I. Skomal, Gregory.
SF458.G6D4 1996
639.3'752—dc20   96-3179
                CIP

Manufactured in the United States of America
10 9 8 7 6 5 4 3 2 1

Series Director: Dominique DeVito
Series Assistant Director: Ariel Cannon
Book Design: Michele Laseau
Cover Design: Iris Jeromnimon
Illustration: Jeff Yesh
Photography:
  Cover photos by Aaron Norman
  Aaron Norman: 2–3, 5, 8, 11, 13, 16, 20, 25, 26, 27, 29, 30, 32, 33, 35, 37, 41,
  46–47, 48, 55, 67, 69, 71, 72, 74, 85, 96, 102, 114, 115, 136, 139, 144
  Fred Rosenzweig: 23, 28, 31, 34, 36, 38, 39, 40, 42, 77, 92–93, 94, 97, 116, 117,
  119, 120, 123, 125
Production Team: Trudy Brown, Jama Carter, Kathleen Caulfield, Trudy Coler,
  Amy De Angelis, Pete Fornatale, Matt Hannafin, Kathy Iwasaki, Vic Peterson,
  Terri Sheehan, Marvin Van Tiem, and Kathleen Varanese

Contents

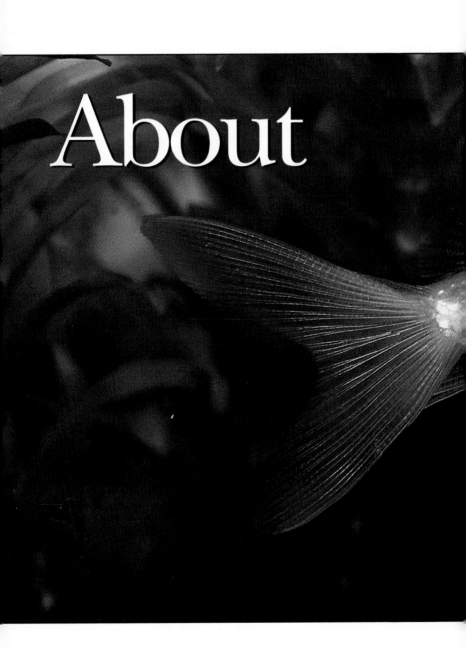

About

part one

Goldfish

External Features of the Goldfish

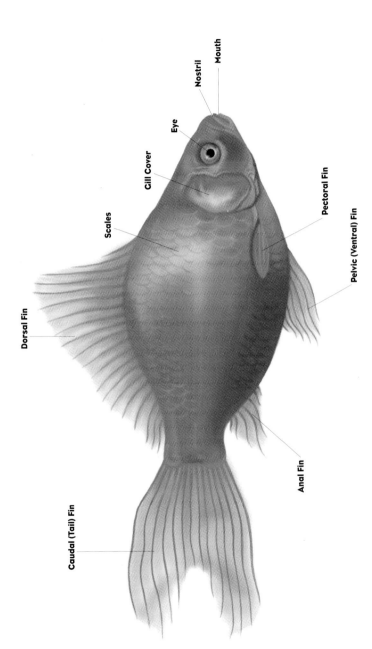

Mouth

Nostril

Eye

Gill Cover

Pectoral Fin

Scales

Pelvic (Ventral) Fin

Dorsal Fin

Anal Fin

Caudal (Tail) Fin

chapter 1

What
Is a
Goldfish?

The popular image of a goldfish in a bowl has been depicted the world over—from Chinese Ming Dynasty pottery to such popular current comic strips as "Garfield." It is a well known fact that Sir Winston Churchill was quite fond of the goldfish he kept at his country residence, Blenheim Palace, palace of the dukes of Marlborough since the seventeenth century.

Goldfish are the most popular domesticated aquatic life in the world and there are over 125 varieties—more varieties than any other fish species.

The History of Goldfish

All of these varieties, it is thought, have been generated from a single species—the Crucian Carp. The goldfish of today are generally more colorful than their ancestors. These carp were long, flat-sided and generally looked like common goldfish, save that the current form has a yellowish, metallic coloring.

The Crucian Carp and its various progeny were peculiar to Asia, and for centuries were particularly prized in China, and, some time later, in Japan. The Chinese word for goldfish is *Chin-yii*. It was in China, during the Tsin Dynasty (A.D. 265–419) that the fish were first mentioned. Some 500 years later, during the Sung Dynasty (A.D. 960–1279) it was not uncommon to have domesticated fish. These were usually kept in ponds or pools in courtyards and the like.

The species was so popular in China, and in Peking especially, that during the second Chin Dynasty (A.D. 415–1234) a goldfish pool was established that was used for commercial breeding in the capital city. Finally, goldfish reached such a height of popularity during the Ming Dynasty (A.D. 1368–1643) that goldfish were housed in clay aquariums and brought inside the home.

The Japanese were also very keen on goldfish, and became quite enamored of these golden creatures. Koriyana has been one of the most famous goldfish-breeding centers for more than 500 years. It was there, in 1704, that San Sanzaemon first established his business, which has spawned an entire industry over the last half of the millennium.

It was between these two main breeding centers and others that developed over the centuries that the Chinese and Japanese bred such variations as the Fantail, the Veiltail, the Globe-Eyed and the transparent-scaled varieties, some of which can be traced as far back as the late sixteenth and early seventeenth centuries.

During the eighteenth century, as trade with the English, French, Dutch and Portuguese flourished, goldfish became fashion gifts and pets throughout England, France and even as far inland as Germany. The first recorded shipment of goldfish imported to America was in 1878, by Admiral Ammon.

According to Anmarie Barrie, a noted writer on goldfish, the keeping of tropical fish became truly popular in the western hemisphere after the opening of the first aquarium to the public, in 1853, at the London Zoo. A chemist named Warrington and a surgeon named Ellis first realized the "relationship between fish, plants and water." The first goldfish show took place in Osaka, Japan, in 1862. The first goldfish show in the West took place in 1926 and was organized by the British Aquarists Association in London.

Despite there being 125 varieties of goldfish, the United States has only contributed one variety to this ever-popular species—that is the Comet. It was bred here by Hugo Murkett and the U.S. Fisheries Department around 1881. While it is the only variety bred on American shores at the time of this writing, with the numerous breeding centers around the nation, America's contribution could grow at any minute.

SLEEPING

If there is quiet time in your house, usually at night, you may find your fish at the bottom of the tank, among some rocks or plants. Since they have no eyelids, many people think the fish are always awake. Wrong! They're asleep! Goldfish tend to lose some color and luster when sleeping at night. Occasionally the pectoral or tail fins will move to keep the fish balanced.

To grow to their potential and have the best color they can develop, it is important that your goldfish have room to exercise and sleep. Goldfish need their rest, just like you, so turn the light off during the evening hours and let your fish sleep. If you don't turn the light off, the fish will sleep for shorter periods of time or largely go without, which could result in shorter life-spans, less color and less active fish. If you are trying to grow or breed your fish, it is imperative that you shut the tank light off at night so that they can get their rest.

Goldfish as Pets

Regardless of variety, the keeping of goldfish is one of the most popular forms of pet ownership in the world. The size of the aquarium can vary, depending on the size of the room, and can be kept with relatively little maintenance. Goldfish don't need to be housebroken, they won't beg at the table and you'll never have to cover up the sofa when you aren't home.

The great thing about goldfish is that they are a fairly hardy species, and are quite adaptable. They are excellent candidates for outdoor ponds or pools, in almost any climate. Given the wide range of colors, body shapes and general disposition, there is in fact a goldfish for everyone.

Any good pet shop owner should tell you, when you are choosing fish, that goldfish should not be kept with tropical fish. Goldfish should be kept with goldfish. Why? There are many reasons.

What's the Difference between Goldfish and Tropical Fish?

All the fins contribute to the goldfish's swimming and maneuvering through water. This Oranda has beautiful, fine fins.

Overall, the goldfish is a hardier species than other tropicals. Goldfish do not require a heater in their tank, and are actually better off if the temperature gets cold for a little while (six to eight weeks). Tropical fish, for the most part, require a consistent temperature, mostly in the high sixties and low seventies, depending on the variety, while goldfish can live in the mid- to low forties. While the goldfish can survive in higher temperatures, they tend to develop some diseases more readily.

Also, goldfish don't get along with other fish. Depending on the variety, the goldfish might be too aggressive or it might be the other fish's lunch. Kept with some community fish, the goldfish might be too territorial. For example, angel fish and goldfish don't get along. But which fish is actually the aggressor depends on which camp you speak to.

Kept with cichlids, it is likely that your goldfish will be gone by morning. Even when kept only with other goldfish, it is important to keep the same types in groups together. Comets and Bubble Eyes would not be good together because the Comets swim faster and would tend to eat more and faster than the Bubble Eyes, which are delicate and need expert handling.

Lastly, given the opportunity, the goldfish will grow significantly larger than many other aquarium fish. There are exceptions, of course, including the Oscar and the Arrowana, both of which feed on small fish once they grow to a certain size.

What's the Difference between Goldfish and Koi?

Koi are a cousin to the carp and the goldfish. As such, there are many things about the Koi that are very similar to the goldfish. Their breeding and feeding habits, and the water temperature they require, are all the same. Koi even have very similar colorations, except that they are in larger patches on the body. However, while the Common Goldfish,the largest of all goldfish, rarely grows larger than twelve to fourteen inches, Koi normally grow to eighteen inches and have been seen as long as almost four feet. Koi need a lot of space and are not good aquarium fish.

The reason most people confuse Koi with goldfish is that they look similar and are both pond fish—Koi even more so. Japanese-bred Koi are thought to be far superior to those bred anywhere else.

The easiest way to distinguish between goldfish and Koi is this: Koi have small nubbly whiskers on the sides of their mouths and underneath the chin. These do not grow very long, but they are noticeable all the same.

The Classification of the Goldfish

Goldfish, known also as the *Carassius auratus,* still can be found in streams and ponds throughout Asia. In the wild their colors are somewhat more muddy. The goldfish comes from the Cyprinidae family, a classification of Carp. They are descended from the Crucian Carp, also known as *Carassius carassius,* and are related to the common carp, which is known as *Cyprinus carpio.*

The best way to distinguish between a carp and a goldfish is to look at the dorsal fin. The goldfish's dorsal is usually straight up or is concave (curved in) while the carp's dorsal is generally convex (curved out).

The Body and Its Structure

There are over 300 different varieties of goldfish. Some of them are unique, and fall outside the general physiognomy of fish altogether. We will use the Comet goldfish as the classic example of a goldfish when we discuss them in general terms. Comets are the common American variety.

The Comet's body is streamlined, being more or less flat on the sides. The view from the top shows the middle as somewhat thicker than the head or tail section. The view from the side shows the middle as somewhat deeper, whereas the body tapers toward the head and the section where the body meets the tail. This narrow section is also known as the caudal peduncle.

Regardless of variety, especially among the fancies, the caudal peduncle is almost always narrow, no matter how large the body. Some Fantails, especially the Redcap and the Marigold Chinese Lionhead, have exceptionally large heads, while Fantail, Moor and Veiltail, which are quite round, vary in their head shapes and sizes. To locate the body parts discussed here, refer to the diagram on page 4.

FINS

Fins have three main functions: stabilization, braking and propulsion. They come in two types, paired and median, and they are located at five places on the fish's body.

The **pectoral** fins are the forwardmost fins, and are an excellent example of paired fins. They are almost always moving, because they help the fish to turn, hover, navigate tight corners or propel backward. While they can help in forward propulsion, it is not their main function. The pectorals are usually found somewhere underneath or just behind and below the gills, on each side, toward the bottom of the body. They are not always shaped the same on different varieties. They can be short and small as on a Lionhead, or long and flowing as on a Veiltail.

The pectoral fins are the forwardmost fins, located below and behind the gills. They're easy to see on this Fantail.

The **dorsal** fin is an excellent example of the median fin. It rises directly from the top of the middle of the fish's back. It is made up of rigid and soft spines webbed with membrane. When a goldfish is healthy, this fin stands straight up, and its main function is to help stabilize the fish. It keeps the fish from rolling over by keeping the bottom of the fish down. Whether

hovering or during forward propulsion, it keeps the
fish moving straight. Some varieties, like the Celestial,
have no dorsal fin, and consequently have more diffi-
culty swimming.

The **pelvic** or **ventral** fins are a pair of fins at the
abdomen, toward the bottom of the fish, generally in
front of the anal canal. More than anything they act as
brakes, but they also stabilize and help in turning.
While ventral or pelvic fins may be elongated, as on a
Veiltail Ryunkin, they rarely grow so large that they
impair or grow beyond use, as opposed to the dorsal
and caudal fins.

The **anal** fin protrudes from the bottom of the body in
front of the anal and sexual openings. It is a median
fin, and its main job is to function as a stabilizer. On
some varieties, these fins can aid in propulsion and
turning in small spaces. Sometimes, in the fancy varieties, the anal fin becomes a set of paired fins.
Interestingly, they grow from the spot where there
would have been a median fin, and are the only set of
paired fins that are actually joined together where they
meet the body. Sometimes the fins themselves are actually joined along the backside of the fin for a short dis-
tance, but never for the length of it.

The **caudal** or **tail** fin is actually a median fin. The
caudal or tail fin is extremely important in propulsion,
and is usually the source for most of the power during
swimming. It can also act as a brake, but is much more
helpful in turning. While fancy varieties might have a
fantail or some other elongated tail, like the anal fin,
it is really a median fin. The fins can sometimes
be forked, as in the Black Moor, or can be wide and
fan-shaped, as in the Veiltail. In the fancier varieties,
these fins are so exaggerated that they are not as
helpful, if at all, and consequently, these fish are bad
swimmers.

There are three different types of caudal fins: the single tail fin, the veiltail and the fantail. There are varieties of each of these, but these are the three main

types. The single tail fin is obvious, and can be found on the common goldfish. The fantail is the most common of the fancy varieties. This is a pair of forked tails joined at the caudal peduncle. The veiltail is a beautiful, large tail, which has no indentations (or forks) and is square finished. It is usually very long and elegant.

SCALES

The body of a goldfish is covered with overlapping *scales*. The scales are composed of a hard, bony substance. They serve to protect the fish, reducing the chance of injuries or infection.

These are covered by epidermal tissue. Numerous glands secrete mucus and produce the slimy effect we view as slippery. The slimy coating helps the fish to swim more easily in the water, reducing the friction between its body and the water itself. The slimy coating also acts to guard against injury or infection.

The scale is actually transparent; the color of the goldfish usually comes from the dermis, the lower or inner layer of skin. The forward end of each scale is attached to the dermis. The scales overlap each other like shingles on a house, providing a solid wall of protection as well as comfortable movement. "The wild form of the goldfish," according to Neil Teitler, a goldfish expert, "has between 28 and 31 scales along the lateral line and 6 scales between the dorsal spine and the lateral line." The lateral line is a series of indentations having to do with the senses and will be discussed later.

The Black Moor exhibits an abundance of melanophores, a type of skin pigment. Notice this fish's long, large veiltail caudal fin.

For every variety of goldfish, the specific number of scales remains the same within that group, from fish to fish. For each season of growth in a goldfish (approximately one year, provided that there is a six- to eight-week drop in temperature), the goldfish develops a ring in its scales. The number of rings on the scale determines the age of the fish. These rings are called *circuli*.

Scale Types   Goldfish can be characterized based on four different kinds of scale groups: metallic, matt, nacreous and calico.

Metallic fish exhibit a shiny, scaly exterior, such as is seen in the Comet. These scales contain a crystalline substance called guanine. Guanine is responsible for the sheen of the scales. The more guanine, the shinier the scale.

Some scales lack guanine almost entirely. They are called *matt* scales and exhibit no reflective tissue anywhere on the fish's body; rather, they have a flat or skinlike look to them. Truly matt-type goldfish are often not available commercially. They lack intensive coloration and do not seem as hardy as other fish. Matt fish are sometimes referred to as scaleless. This is incorrect—there is no such thing as a scaleless goldfish.

When metallic- and matt-type scales are both found on a goldfish it is known as *nacreous*. Some individual scales, or whole sections of the body, might feature a metallic-type finish, while others might feature a matt-type finish.

Many feel that *calico* is really a part of the nacreous group. This category has gained popularity, as it classifies any goldfish with three or more colors appearing anywhere on the body.

COLOR

The *coloration* of a goldfish, or any fish for that matter, depends on a wide variety of circumstances. Water composition and temperature greatly affect a fish's chromatophores (pigment cells), as do diet and environment. There are two types of chromatophores: melanophores and xanthophores. Orange goldfish exhibit an abundance of xanthophores and an absence of melanophores, while the blue or black varieties, such as a Black Moor, have an abundance of melanophores and lack xanthophores.

SWIM BLADDER

A swim bladder is a gas-filled sac that helps a goldfish rise or fall in its watery environment. In a goldfish, there are actually two swim bladders, one directly in front of the other. These compartments contain oxygen, carbon dioxide and nitrogen.

By inflating the swimbladder the goldfish rises; conversely, when the goldfish deflates the swimbladder, descent is made easier. This also helps the fish stabilize and hover comfortably. Some of the more elaborate varieties are top-heavy, and as a result, will always swim at an angle. An example of this is the Lionhead, which has a smaller forward sac, causing its head to thrust slightly at a downward angle.

The swim bladder is more notorious for the ailment it causes—swim bladder disease. Afflicted fish swim on their sides at the top, or conversely, sink to the bottom. Some also lose their sense of balance and might somersault as they attempt to swim forward. This is sometimes caused by changes in temperature that most often occur in fish transportation. Swim bladder disease is a digestive problem. Detected and diagnosed early, it is treatable by isolation and medicated food. However, it is not a contagious disease. Detected too late, the results are irreversible—it is a deadly disease.

Other Organs   Although goldfish are different from tropical fishes in terms of anatomy, they possess circulatory, respiratory, digestive and nervous systems common to most members of this vertebrate group.

How Do Goldfish Swim?

The back-and-forth movement of the tail fin provides the goldfish with forward motion. The fish literally pulls the tail from one side of its body to the other. By going back and forth, the tail pushes the water behind it, thus pushing the fish forward. By bending the tail appropriately, the fish also steers itself.

The dorsal fin keeps the fish right-side up, and the pectoral, ventral and anal fins help to thrust and steer, as well as stop. The pectoral fins are used for tight turning and hovering.

The fish stops by reversing the tail motion, quickly. All other fins immediately become rigid. Sometimes the pectoral fins are instrumental in backing up and are at times used when a quick or sudden stop is needed, much like a thruster rocket on a spaceship.

The beautiful double-tailed Oranda is a favorite breed of goldfish.

How Do Goldfish Breathe?

Goldfish, like all fish, require oxygen to live. Since they live in the water they do not breathe as we do. Instead of lungs, they have gills. These organs extract oxygen from the water and expel carbon dioxide from their own system, much like other vertebrates. As the fish swims, it opens its mouth, taking in vast amounts of water. An oral membrane automatically closes off the water from going down the proverbial wrong pipe.

The water passes through the gills, which in the goldfish are located on either side of the head. The gills are filled with tiny membranes.

As the water passes over these membranes and filaments, oxygen is exchanged for carbon dioxide. As the blood passes through the filaments, they oxygenate the blood while releasing all the other unwanted gases. This is called osmosis. A minute amount of breathing takes place through the skin.

When there is insufficient oxygen in the water, fish rise to just below the surface, their mouths actually protruding from the water, gulping for air. These fish are actually trying to avoid suffocation. This circumstance most often occurs in the well-known "goldfish bowl." We will talk about the dangers and problems of the goldfish bowl in another chapter.

A Goldfish's Senses

Smell   A goldfish has nostrils called *nares*. But unlike us, who breathe through our noses, goldfish cannot. Their nostrils, located above the mouth and below the eyes, are really only small pits of scent buds. These are not attached to the respiratory system, but rather, via a nerve, are connected to the brain.

The sense of smell is strong with goldfish, and is highly important in the search for food and in mating. Water enters the nostril and is passed over membranes. It is then passed out the same way it came in. Sometimes contaminated water can disorient a fish, making finding food or mating difficult.

Taste   Most of a goldfish's tastebuds are located on the lips and all over the mouth. There are even tastebuds on the outsides of the lips. This is an advantage for the goldfish in the hunt for food and for a mate. Goldfish have no tongues.

Touch   Lateral line adaptations give the goldfish the best sense of what we mean when we say touch. The lateral line is a series of dimples in somewhat of a line across the fish's side. These dimples are thermosensory nerve endings connected to the brain, and when pressure is exerted on them, or when vibrations occur, the fish can feel them right away.

Hearing Goldfish have no outward ears. Their hearing lies entirely inside the skull. They have a pair of membranous sacs, each of which is composed of two chambers, the *utriculus* or *dorsal sacs* and the *sacculus* or *ventral sacs*.

Sound vibrations pass through the water, through the fish's body, and reverberate in this inner ear. The sacculus contains the *earstone* or *otolith*. It is this complex that gives a goldfish its sense of hearing, and like our own inner ear, its sense of balance. We know for sure that fish make sounds during eating, fighting and mating, and hear intruders when being attacked. Hearing is an essential tool for goldfish survival.

Vision The eyes of fish operate somewhat like our own, except that they lack eyelids and their irises work much slower than our own. That is why if the light is turned on suddenly, fish seem to go into shock. Because it takes their eyes longer to adjust to the change in light, they are temporarily blinded. Their eyes eventually adjust, though it may take a couple of hours.

Also, fish have flat corneas and flat-shaped lenses, causing them to be particularly nearsighted. This is not a great handicap, since visibility in ponds and lakes is not always very good. Also, since these fish were bred for hobbyists, nearsighted vision is all that is really required.

On the other hand, goldfish are able to detect color. Also, since their eyes are on either side of their heads, they have monocular vision as opposed to binocular vision like us (which we find useful in judging distances). Goldfish eyes have little movement.

The eyes are efficient at spotting food and dangers, including other fish. Highly developed goldfish varieties, which have bubble eyes or telescope eyes, are thought to see only upward. The Bubble Eye variety, which develops large, fluid sacs underneath its eyes, is believed to suffer vision loss as well, but no one can be sure. There are cases of other species, tropical fish, that have no eyes at all and live full lives. However, the above-mentioned goldfish strains, when maintained with ordinary care, suffer no great problems when housed with other fish of the same type.

Getting Along with Each Other

Generally speaking, goldfish are not aggressive when kept with other goldfish of the same type. They, like all fish, tend to pick on injured or much smaller goldfish in the same tank, especially if they are crowded. Generally they are active and hardy fish, save a few of the more exotic species, like the Bubble Eyes, which require expert handling. In ponds or pools, like many fish, goldfish tend to school very easily. In these fish, there is never a lead goldfish—the school merely darts around following at whimsy one fish or another.

Goldfish do tend to be aggressive during breeding time. However, there are no challenges or fights between males for the right to mate with a female goldfish. Male goldfish will merely chase any female down until they eventually get their chance to spawn.

Classification of the Goldfish and Its Near Relatives

Super-Class:	Gnathostomata (Jawed fish)	
Class:	Osteichthyes (Bony Fish)	
Sub-Class:	Actinopterygii	
Infra-Class:	Teleostei	
Order:	Cypriniformes (Carp-like fish and Characins)	
Sub-Order:	Cyprinioidei (Approximately 2,000 species in six families)	
Family:	Cyprinidae	
Genus:	Carassius	Cyprinus
Species:	C. Carassius (Crucian Carp)	C. Carpio (Common Carp)
	C. Auratus (Goldfish)	

chapter 2

Selecting
Your
Goldfish

There are tell-tale signs you should look for when selecting your fish, no matter what variety. These tips should be strictly adhered to, as you do not need to buy a diseased fish right from the start.

Signs of a Healthy Goldfish

Activity Level This is the most important thing to look for. You want healthy, active fish that swim smoothly, are capable of quick reactions and seem alert to their surroundings. You should not buy a fish that is either always at the top or the bottom of the tank, that is swimming on its side or that is upside-down. Any fish that looks as though it's having trouble swimming should be avoided.

Eyes   Never let someone sell you a fish that has cloudy eyes, cataracts, or any other kind of mutation of the eyes unless that person is an expert in that breed. A goldfish's eyes should be bright, clear, and unclouded, and the fish should react to light.

Fins   Including the tail fin, the fish's fins should be erect or upright and intact. They should almost always be fanned out. You should not buy a fish with any spots of fungus anywhere on its fins, and there should be no frayed, split or folded surfaces.

Scales   If there are any signs of fungus, white or otherwise, any wounds or any missing scales, don't buy the fish. Fish should have unblemished bodies, with no missing scales and no hints of disease.

One Variety or a Mixture?

Keep in mind that all goldfish have been bred from the *Carassius auratus,* or the common goldfish. All goldfish are basically a variation on two or three body types. There are the sleeker fish, like the Comet (common goldfish); the egg-shaped goldfish, like the Pearl-Scale; and the egg-shaped goldfish without dorsal fins, like the Ranchu. Basically, all the variations on these have at one time or another been bred with all the other varieties, creating one more variety for each new fish. For example, almost every new variety has several basic colorations, including orange metallic, a calico variety, and a Tancho variety.

Remember, depending on what variety you decide on, you should keep to the same group type. For example, if you decided to raise Lionheads, you should not pair them with Comets. Comets are long, sleek and excellent swimmers. Lionheads are short and round and have no dorsal fins. The Comet is extremely hardy and competitive where food is concerned; the Lionhead is among the slowest of goldfish and would not do well paired with the Comet.

As you read on, you will understand more and more about the various types of goldfish and understand the differences more clearly. They are things you will need to consider when choosing the fish you want for your aquarium.

Mixing Other Species with Goldfish

The real difference between goldfish and tropical fish is their ability to live in various water temperatures. The Comet can live in water temperatures ranging from 40°F to 80°F. Most tropical fish need water temperatures in the 72°F to 85°F range.

However, compatibility is important. Goldfish and tropical fish do not mix well. One group or the other will become aggressive, and the end result will be a badly injured or dead fish. The benefit of choosing goldfish is that there are more than 300 different varieties, providing a range of choice available in no other breed.

Another thing to remember is never to place perch, sunfish or any other natural wildlife in with your goldfish. These are fresh cold water fish, but are generally more aggressive and stronger than goldfish.

Avoid Overcrowding

Goldfish are very hardy fish. They are generally very active and are capable of growing quite large. The common goldfish can grow more than a foot long! The acknowledged rule is one inch of fish for each gallon of water. But you can't keep a twelve-inch goldfish in a twelve-gallon tank. When selecting the number of goldfish you want, you should keep in mind how big an aquarium you are choosing. This will determine the number (see the accompanying box).

HOW TO AVOID OVERCROWDING

In order to avoid overcrowding, it is important to keep the proper number of fish for the number of gallons of water in your tank. You should use this information as a guide when setting up your aquarium.

GALLONS OF WATER	NUMBER OF COLDFISH
1	1
5	2–3
10	3–4
20	6–8
30	9–12

Overcrowding will result in bad water conditions, and it will be difficult to supply enough aerated water in your tank for the number of fish. The idea is to create an environment that is beneficial to the fish, not to pack as many fish into as small a place as possible. The more space per goldfish, the healthier and more active they will be.

Pay particular attention to the eyes when selecting your goldfish. They should not look cloudy as they do here. This fish is blind.

Keeping the Bottom of the Tank Clean

If you're wondering if you need a catfish to keep the bottom of your tank clean, the short answer is no. Goldfish are excellent bottom feeders, constantly scouting the aquarium floor for available food. In the end, goldfish will do the job themselves. Also, many tropical catfish are not able to withstand the colder temperatures goldfish prefer. Cold, freshwater catfish are not a good idea since some have been known to suck the eyes out of the fancier goldfish varieties. No one knows why.

Do you need snails? Not really. Again, goldfish are excellent scavengers all by themselves. What do you need a snail for? You don't. Having snails in your aquarium will bring on more problems than it cures.

chapter 3

The
Varieties
of Goldfish

There are no official divisions among varieties of goldfish, but there are several different groupings of goldfish one should understand before beginning.

It is important to group these fish together in the same way you would set up an aquarium for a beginner, or, for that matter, an experinced fish enthusiast or an expert. In fact, these are the groups that have been suggested by pet store owners nationwide and acknowledged by goldfish enthusiasts.

For example, the Comet, the Common Goldfish and the Shubunkin (both Bristol and London types) are all in the same category. These are strong, hardy swimmers, competitive fish, and should definitely not be kept with a Lionhead or Veiltail, as these are slower swimmers and will not be able to compete for food at the same level. Consult your local pet store owner before pairing unlike fish.

The following is a small sampling of the many different types of goldfish available, but many of the most commercially available are included, as well those that are actually quite rare.

Body Type and Finnage

There are two basic goldfish body types. The first is the *flat* body type, including the Common Goldfish, the Comet and the Shubunkin. The second is the *round* or *egg-shaped* body type, like the Oranda and the Veiltail. However, there is a second group within the egg-shaped group that lack a dorsal fin, like the Lionhead and the Celestial. The distinction here is very important. Goldfish that lack a dorsal fin do not swim as well as their cousins with dorsal fins. A Fantail is a better swimmer than a Lionhead, and would be more likely to get the "lion's share" of the food, etc. These are always very important considerations in setting up goldfish.

SINGLE-TAIL, FLAT-BODIED GOLDFISH

These types of goldfish are among the hardiest of all goldfish families. They are the fastest swimmers and are the most streamlined. As a result they are very competitive and successful in the hunt for food as compared with more exotic species. They all tend to be extremely easy to care for, and are excellent choices for beginners. These are also the breeds that tend to be better for ponds and the group that tends to grow the largest.

The Common Goldfish is the hardiest of all goldfish. Its life expectancy is somewhere between five and ten years if properly maintained. It can withstand temperatures as low as 40°F and as high as 80°F. These are ideal candidates for outdoor ponds, as they are able to withstand great temperature changes.

Long, sleek and flat-bodied, the Common Goldfish is the closest cousin in the goldfish family to the carp. When young, they tend to be a bluish color. As they age, goldfish will turn to a metallic orange.

The Common Goldfish is tapered at the head and caudal peduncle, is flat-bodied and is wider in the middle. It is deeper in height and wider in width than the Comet. Its fins are classic: an erect dorsal fin, a single forked tail, well-proportioned pectoral and ventral fins. They are not overly large fins, but rather just what is necessary. These goldfish are fast swimmers and very competitive. In a pond they can grow as large as twelve to fourteen inches, and in a large aquarium six to nine inches, depending on the size of the tank.

The Comet is the only goldfish to have originated in the United States. It was developed in the 1880s by the U.S. Fisheries Department. At about the same time, Hugo Mulrett, an American breeder, developed what happened to be the same type of strain. It is Mr. Mulrett who gave the Comet its name. In Japan it is called *tetsugyo*. Comets were placed in the reflecting pond on the Mall in Washington, D.C.

The Comet looks very much like a Common Goldfish, except that it is generally longer and sleeker, and has more exaggerated fins. The fins are approximately twice as long as those of a Common Goldfish, but the fin types are the same. The tail fin is especially large and beautiful, sometimes as large or larger than the body. It has the same metallic orange color as well. Comets come in silver (white) and yellow, as well as in combinations of these colors. While they are usually metallic, nacreous Comets are not at all uncommon.

Like the Common Goldfish, the Comet is a fast swimmer and is very hardy, able to withstand great changes in temperature, from as low as 40°F to as high as 80°F. Comets are excellent pond or aquarium fish. The Comet is somewhat smaller than the Common Goldfish, and in a pond will only grow to about seven to ten inches in length.

27

There are two types of Shubunkins, the London and the Bristol.

Originally thought to be bred in Japan around the turn of the century, these fish became very popular in England. The name Shubunkin is Japanese, and means deep red with different colors.

Basically the Shubunkin is a common Western goldfish that is calico or nacreous. They are long, sleek and flat-sided. Their most attractive feature is the variety of hues in which they appear. The colors are mostly deep reds, yellows, whites, and dark blues, violets or blacks. It is often said that the more dark hues a Shubunkin has (violets, blues or blacks), the more valuable it is in the marketplace. In some circles, this fish is also known as the Harlequin.

The difference between the Bristol and the London type of Shubunkin is that the Bristol's tail fin is much larger than the London's tail. The Bristol's is a forked, wide tail, but not very long, while the more popular London variety has a smaller, more squared-off tail.

Shubunkins tend to grow to a maximum size of six inches long, and are excellent swimmers. They are very strong and require room to swim. With proper care, the Shubunkin is one of the most long-lived of

all domestic fish, living sometimes between ten and
twenty years. They are ideal for outdoor pools and
ponds and are hardy enough to suffer great temperature changes within a year's cycle.

The Wakin

The Wakin is the common goldfish of Japan, and
Wakin is its Japanese name. This variety was first developed in China, so the name is very tongue-in-cheek.
Bluish in color when very young, it will grow to a deep
vermillion red. Some strains of this variety have white
patches. In all respects it is very much like the common
Western goldfish that we know, except that it has a double caudal or tail fin. Despite their double tail, the
Wakin swim fast enough to be kept with single-tail, flat-
bodied fish.

The Jikin

The Jikin is known more commonly as the Butterfly
Tail Goldfish. It is also known as the Peacock-Tailed
Goldfish. It is very similar to the Wakin in all respects,
and is thought to be bred from the Wakin. The easily
understood difference is the tail. When fully opened, it
forms a large X, and looks very much like a butterfly.
These are hardy fish and are good starter fish, but are
not as easily found as Common or Comets.

There is little difference between this breed and the Comet, except for coloration. The Tancho has a bright-red cap, and its body is usually silver or white. Pink can sometimes be found on the body or on the fins. The forked tail of a Tancho is also smaller than the Comet's.

The name *Tancho* comes from the Japanese crane, which has a red spot on its head. Many breeds have a Tancho coloration, including koi.

ROUND OR EGG-SHAPED BODY TYPE
Dorsal-finned Goldfish

The next two groups hold some of the more exotic varieties in the entire fish lexicon, tropical fish included. They include a numbing variety of tails, body shapes, eye shapes, head shapes, etc. You can see how one's fascination with goldfish alone can easily last a lifetime.

The round or egg-shaped varieties look just like what is suggested here: They look like an egg with fins. They have short, rounded bodies, and it is difficult to distinguish head from body in some varieties.

This group tends to represent the moderate swimmers. They are faster than some more exotic varieties, but not as fast as their more streamlined cousins. What this group lacks in streamlined form, it makes up for in exaggerated finnage and bright bold colorings.

The other thing to remember is that this group, save the Fantail and the Black Moor (depending on where you live), is really not suitable for most outdoor ponds or pools. They tend to need slightly warmer water, and some are not as hardy as the previous group's fishes.

The Fantail

Dating back some 1,300 to 1,500 years, the Fantail is one of the oldest goldfish varieties known to man. The Fantail is called *loochoo* in Chinese, and its metallic orange color should grow very deep and bright.

Shaped like an egg, this fish has a large, double caudal or tail fin. The tail should be long and flowing. The Fantail is the most common fancy breed available to the average hobbyist. And it is also the most popular, outselling all other fancy breeds. The body is the most streamlined of the entire final two groupings, and is still more roundish in shape.

In the best specimens of the breed the fish's tail should not be joined at any juncture along either side, but rather only at the caudal peduncle. The anal fins should be paired as well and, again, not joined in any place, but should be matching and on separate sides.

The most popular Fantails are the solid-orange metallic. They are the most plentiful and the hardiest. The Fantail is also available in nacreous; again, those showing the most blues and blacks are considered to be among the most prized. Nacreous Fantails are not as hardy as their orange metallic relations.

This is the only one of the fancy breeds that is durable and hardy enough for outdoor ponds. It is also the first fancy variety any hobbyist should own before moving into the more exotic breeds. With good care, a Fantail will grow to three to six inches in length, and has a life expectancy of somewhere between five and ten years.

The Nymph

These were popular for some time, but have recently fallen out of favor. It is thought that these goldfish were a cross between a Comet and a Fantail. The Nymph has a short body, is roundish with a deep belly and a short head and has a large mouth with full lips and erect nostrils. It has extremely long fins, and a dorsal fin that sits far back on the spine. Its pectoral and ventral fins are long, as is its single anal fin. The Nymph comes in single-tail, fantail and fringe-tailed varieties.

The Ryunkin is the Japanese version of the Fantail. Some argue that it is the older version of the Fantail. Legend has it that they were first developed on the Ryuku Islands, hence the name. The main difference is that this variety has a high, arching back, from which the dorsal fin extends even higher.

The back appears almost like a hump, which begins just after the head. Also, the tail is wider, meaning that it becomes longer vertically instead of horizontally. Because of the body shape, the fins sometimes appear more toward a right angle than the average Fantail.

The Ryunkin can grow to between three and six inches long and will live five to ten years. Ryunkins are available in all the same color variations as the average Fantail, including Tancho. Ryunkins are also excellent beginner fish for anyone wanting to move toward keeping the more exotic breeds. They are also good for outdoor ponds or pools.

The origin of the Veiltail is somewhat under debate. Some claim, like Anmarie Barrie and John Coborn, both goldfish experts, that the Veiltail is actually a mutation of the Fantail, while Marshall Ostow, another goldfish authority, claims that the Veiltail was bred from the Wakin, the Japanese common goldfish. Regardless, the Veiltail looks more like a Fantail to the novice and for description's sake.

The most striking feature of the Veiltail is the finnage. The dorsal fin extends very high, usually straight up on a good specimen. All the other fins—the pectoral, the paired anal and the caudal—are long and extend in beautiful flowing ribbons downward. It has a double caudal fin and its paired anal fins extend so far back that they are even with the middle of the elongated tail. There are no forks in the tail.

Easily considered one of the most beautiful of all goldfish, these are not the hardiest of fish. They are not the most delicate, but they do need more care than the average goldfish. They require space to swim because of their long finnage, so the aquarium should not be overcrowded with other fish or too many plants. The quality of the water must be maintained, so that they don't lose their color. Their fins are very susceptible to rot and any number of fungal diseases.

The colorations of Veiltails range from orange and red metallic to black to nacreous. The rounder the body, the more ball-shaped, the better that specimen is thought to be.

They will live somewhere between four and six years and will grow to somewhere between three and five inches long, not including the length of the tail. The water they are kept in should be somewhat warmer than for some of the previous breeds mentioned: Don't let the water drop less than 50°F. Ideally, it should be kept somewhere between 65°F and 75°F.

Veiltails are not very competitive and should be kept only with other Veiltails. They are for a more experienced hobbyist. They are not for pond or outdoor use.

The Oranda

The Oranda is the result of crossing a Veiltail Goldfish with a Lionhead Goldfish. Some people call this breed the fantailed lionhead, because it looks as if it comes from Fantail stock, but this is a misnomer. In Japanese it is called the *oranda shishigashira,* which translated means "rare Lionhead." The calico Oranda is called *azumanishiki.*

Like the Lionhead Goldfish (one of those without a dorsal fin), the Oranda has a bumpy growth over

35

its head that resembles a wart. This high head growth, on good specimens, covers the head completely like a cap. This growth, however, should not cover the eyes, nostrils or mouth of the fish. The growth does not even begin to show until these fish are somewhere between two and three years old. The Oranda body is egg-shaped and has long, flowing dual caudal and dual anal fins. The dorsal fin is the same as on a Veiltail.

Mostly available in the orange metallic variety, this head growth takes on the more concentrated coloration of orange. However, in nacreous coloration the growth may be white, orange, red, yellow, black, blue or calico. Again, the more blues and blacks, the more valuable the fish is thought to be. There is even a red cap or Tancho variety of Oranda, which is very striking and among the most highly prized, as its white body provides a stark contrast to the bright cherry-red cap or hood that covers the head.

This fish has a life expectancy of approximately five to ten years, and should be kept at a relatively constant temperature somewhere around 65°F. Given enough room, an Oranda will grow to between three and four inches long, the length of the tail not included. Disease and fungus are sometimes a problem, as these tend to ferment in the folds and crevices of the cap. This fish should only be kept by someone who has experience with goldfish—it is definitely not for the beginner. The Oranda is not for a year-round outdoor pond.

The Pearl-Scale

This is a variety that is growing in popularity. Essentially it looks like a Fantail, except that it is shorter and fatter, somewhat like a Ryunkin, but with less exaggerated finnage. Its back arches high and its dorsal fin begins just forward of the peak of what looks like a hunchback. The abdomen protrudes much deeper

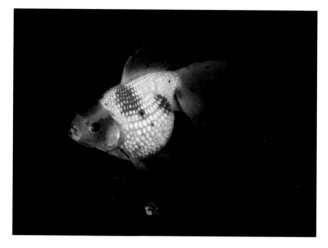

than on almost any of the egg-shaped breeds, making
the body large and ball-like. The caudal fin can sometimes develop into square veiltails.

The Pearl-Scale Goldfish is known for its odd scales,
which seem almost spherical. There is a hard raised
area in the center of each scale. These raised areas are
usually white, and give the impression of pearls stick-
ing out of the fish's body. The larger the scales, it is
thought, the better the quality of the breed. An exceptional specimen will exhibit these scales all the way up
the body to the dorsal fin. The scales, when they fall off
from rubbing, fights or injury of any kind, grow back,
but in a flat, normal variation. These "defects" are not
passed on in breeding no matter when the injuries
occur.

This fish has a life expectancy of approximately five to
ten years, and should be kept at a relatively constant
temperature somewhere between 49°F and 65°F, probably more toward the high end. Given enough room, a
Pearl-Scale Goldfish will grow to be the size of a base-
ball or bigger, not including the fins. Disease and fungus are sometimes a problem, as these tend to ferment
in the folds and crevices of the skin. Good aeration
of the water is necessary to keep the fish healthy for
some time.

The word *demekin* means "goldfish with the protruding eyes" in Japanese. This variety has been known in China since the eighteenth century, according to the goldfish expert Marshall Ostrow, who claims that it was also known as the Dragon Fish or Dragon-eyed Goldfish. In England it is known as the Pop-eyed Goldfish. These Globe-eyed or Telescope-eyed Goldfish are known for their eyes, which protrude in almost tubelike fashion, in adults sometimes in lengths up to three quarters of an inch. The term "telescope" is an anomaly, since these fish have limited vision. There are four different eye shapes in the globe- or telescope-eyed varieties.

In body type and finnage—a short, round, egg-shaped body with double anal and caudal fins—they most resemble the Fantail. Their coloration ranges from orange metallic to nacreous, with combinations similar to those usually found in Fantails. The matt version of these fish is extremely rare. There is a Veiltail version of the Telescope-eyed variety available as well.

This fish has a life expectancy of approximately five to ten years, and should be kept at a relatively constant temperature somewhere between 49°F and 65°F. You should probably err toward the warmer. Given enough room, a Telescope- or Globe-eyed Goldfish will grow to somewhere between four and six inches long, the length of the tail not included. Disease and fungus are sometimes a problem, as the eyes are very delicate and sensitive.

At an early age they do not have a problem with competition for food because their eyes have not yet begun to grow. However, as these fish get older (at around six months to a year in age), their eyes begin to protrude, limiting their vision and putting them at a disadvantage. It has been recommended that this type of fish be kept with its own kind or with other similarly handicapped fish. This fish should only be kept by someone who has experience with goldfish—it is definitely not for the beginner. These types of goldfish are not suitable for ponds.

The Black Moor

The Black Moor is basically an all-black version of the Telescope- or Globe-eyed Goldfish. It is known solely for its color, which appears as a velvetlike black coat. The telescoped eyes are a little larger and less prone to infection than the normal Telescope-eyed Goldfish.

Other than the Fantail, the Black Moor is the only round or egg-shaped goldfish that is hardy enough to survive in outdoor ponds, depending on where you live. Consult your local pet store owner. And, again, like the Fantail, the Black Moor does not make for a bad starter goldfish, because it is so hardy.

The Black Moor has a life expectancy of approximately five to ten years, and should be kept at a relatively constant temperature somewhere between 49°F and 65°F. You should probably err toward the cooler. As Black Moors get older they develop a velvety texture. However, if the water is consistently too warm, orange will sometimes begin to show through. Once this happens, there is usually no going back. Given enough room, a Black Moor will grow to somewhere between four and six inches long, the length of the tail not included.

Dorsal-less Goldfish: The Exotics

Dorsal-less goldfish are the final grouping of goldfish because they are the worst swimmers in the goldfish family. Without a dorsal fin, which is a stabilizing fin, it is difficult for them to mount any speed. They are not as fast, nor are they as quick to turn, as even the slow-moving Veiltails or the Telescope- or Globe-eyed Goldfish.

This group tends to have some of the most exotic of all the goldfish and, as a result, many of these are not recommended for beginners. These fish require the care and maintenance that are only part of the experienced hobbyist's knowledge. None of the fish in this final group is suitable for outdoor ponds or pools.

This is the simplest of all the Lionhead-type varieties. It is a roundish, egg-shaped fish with no dorsal fin. In Japan it is most commonly called *Maruko,* which means "round fish." This is a common name given to a number of fish, but the word seems most closely identified with this breed. Its back is a graceful arch all the way to the caudal peduncle, which is pointed downward. This arch results in a tail that is generally pointed downward as well, at approximately a 45° angle. The finnage is usually short and includes a dual caudal or tail fin.

The most notable feature on this fish, however, is the head, which is covered with a type of cap or hood. Many goldfish experts can only liken the bumpy, fleshy covering to a raspberry in texture. This is an extremely appropriate comparison. Neither hard nor soft, this fleshy cap is what gives the Ranchu, and its relations, notoriety.

The cap doesn't even begin to appear on most specimens until their second year. The cap or hood may grow until the fish is a little over three years old. Because the cap sometimes impairs the fish's breathing, the water in its tank must be well aerated.

There are three types of growth as considered by the Japanese: *Tokin,* when the growth takes place just above the head, and results in a look that resembles a cap; *Okame,* when the growth covers the sides of the head, with no growth on top, giving the impression of swollen or stuffed cheeks; and *Shishigashira,* which is a full hood, covering the top of the head, the sides of the head and the opercular areas as well.

These fish come in metallic and nacreous forms, and are seen in combinations of orange, red, yellow, silver, white, blue, violet and black. As usual in calico variations, the more blues and blacks, the more valuable the fish is thought to be.

This fish has a life expectancy of approximately five to ten years, and should be kept at a relatively constant temperature somewhere around 55°F to 65°F. Given enough room, a Ranchu will grow to somewhere between two and three inches long, the length of the tail not included. Disease and fungus are sometimes a problem, as these tend to ferment in the folds and crevices of the cap. This fish should only be kept by someone who has experience with goldfish and is definitely not for the beginner.

The Lionhead is the Chinese version of the Ranchu. The head growth tends to be more encompassing and much more pronounced. The Lionhead also tends to average between one-half to one inch longer than the Ranchu. The Lionhead is also larger in body width, not being as streamlined as the Ranchu.

The Lionhead has a larger, broader back and head to begin with, and is sometimes thought to be boxier. The dual tail tends to be a little larger and more pronounced. It is this larger, more obvious hood that gives the fish its name, the fleshy cap resembling a lion's mane. The Lionhead is much more popular in America than the Ranchu.

These fish are also known as Brambleheads, Buffalo-Heads or Tomato-Heads.

These fish are not the best of swimmers. Because of their body structure or form, they tend to swim forward at a downward angle. Some experts cite the lack of a dorsal fin for this feature, while others note the swimbladder location or the size of the cap. Regardless, this is not one of the more competitive goldfish, and should not be kept with Comets or Shubunkins, for example. Even a Fantail is probably not a good companion for a Lionhead, no matter the sizes or differences in age. You should ask your local pet store owner for his or her advice on your mixture of goldfish.

This fish has a life expectancy of approximately five to ten years, and should be kept at a relatively constant temperature somewhere between 55°F and 65°F. Given enough room, a Lionhead will grow to somewhere between three and four inches long, the length of the tail not included. Disease and fungus are sometimes a problem, as these tend to ferment in the folds and crevices of the cap. This fish should only be kept by an experienced hobbyist.

The Marigold Chinese Lionhead

As the name might suggest, this is nothing more than a variation of the Lionhead. These are also known as Sunrises. The distinguishing feature of these fish is an extremely pronounced hood. It is so large that its yellow color makes it look very much like a marigold flower. The fish are completely colored in a bright yellow. They are extremely rare, and usually not available in commercial pet shops, but must be specially ordered. They tend to be somewhat more delicate, too, than ordinary Lionheads.

The Pompon's body is short and boxy like a Lionhead, except that the growth on the head is different. The Pompon's nasal septum (also known as narial flaps) is so enlarged that it grows outward, so that there are two tassels or pompons. These are called "narial bouquets," and are basically skin flaps folded over and over.

This growth is somewhat softer than the cap that grows on a Lionhead or a Ranchu. The growth has a velvety appearance that sways when the fish swims. This variety is also known by the names Velvetball and Velvetyball. The growths are very susceptible to disease and fungus, and are easily damaged. Older Pompon do develop *tokin,* a caplike head growth similar to the Ranchu.

The most popular breeds of this fish are of the orange dorsal-less type. However, there are also Pompon Orandas, Lionhead Pompons and the Hanafusa, which is the dorsaled version of the same fish. These are not normally available to the average consumer.

These fish come in metallic and nacreous, and are seen in combinations of orange, red, yellow, silver, white, blue, violet and black. As usual in calico variations, the more blues and blacks, the more valuable the fish is thought to be.

45

This fish has a life expectancy of approximately five to ten years, and should be kept at a relatively constant temperature somewhere between 55°F and 65°F. Given enough room, a Pompon will grow to somewhere between three and four inches long, the length of the tail not included.

Brocaded Goldfish

Known as Kinranshi in Japan, this fish is thought to be a hybrid of a Lionhead and a Ryunkin. The body resembles that of the Wakin while the finnage, especially the lack of a dorsal fin, reminds one of a Lionhead. Its mottling is a rich gold color mixed with black, red and white, just like gold brocade, from whence it gets its name. It was first bred in 1905 in Japan by Akiyama Kichigoro.

Celestial

It has been put forward by Niel Teitier that the Celestial was developed in Korea in the late 1700s, and was not bred in Japan or China until after the turn of this century. However, Marshall Ostrow seems to think that this fish, which he says the Chinese named Stargazer, was bred in China first. He appears to believe that it was the Japanese who "locked its eyes forever on the heavens." Regardless, the Japanese

call it Deme-ranchu. It is also known by the names Chiutien Ngarn and Chotengan.

The Celestial is so named because its eyes point skyward. The eyes are positioned on top of outgrowths, rather than at the ends. This growth begins at a very early age. The eyes are held in strong casings. Since these goldfish are only able to see upward, their forward and lateral vision is poor. Celestials tend to feel their way around or position themselves in the direction they want to see. In a good specimen, one should find the fish's eyes pointed in the same direction, with pupils of the same size.

The Celestial is somewhat more streamlined than its other dorsal-less cousins. However, it is still close in likeness to the Lionhead or the Ranchu.

These fish come in metallic and nacreous, and are seen in combinations of orange, red, yellow, silver, white, blue, violet and black. As usual in calico variations, the more blues and blacks, the more valuable the fish is thought to be.

This fish has a life expectancy of approximately five to ten years, and should be kept at a relatively constant temperature somewhere between 55°F and 65°F. Given enough room, a Celestial Goldfish will grow to somewhere between four and six inches long, the length of the tail not included. Disease and fungus are sometimes a problem, as the eyes are very delicate and sensitive.

These goldfish are known for the large fluid-filled sacs that grow underneath each eye. The eye itself is quite normal; however, in almost half the cases, the sacs grow so tight and large that the eyes begin to point upward like those of a Celestial. The sacs should always be of the same size. They are very delicate and are prone to injury, but they do repair themselves. When the fish swims these sacs bounce, giving them a precarious look.

Bubble-eyes have a body like a Celestial, which is to say that they have a longer, sleeker body than a Lionhead or Ranchu, but are nowhere near a Comet or Common Goldfish. They have a dual caudal fin. And, of course, they are dorsal-less. Unlike the Pompon, the Ranchu and the Lionhead, they develop no other growth on their head at any time.

These fish come in metallic and nacreous, and are seen in combinations of red, orange, yellow, silver, white, blue, violet and black. As usual in calico variations, the more blues and blacks, the more valuable the fish is thought to be.

This fish has a life expectancy of approximately five to ten years, and should be kept at a relatively constant temperature somewhere between 55°F and 65°F. Given enough room, a Bubble-eyed Goldfish will grow to somewhere between three and five inches long, the length of the tail not included. Disease and fungus are sometimes a problem, as the eyes are very delicate and sensitive. All sharp objects should be removed from the tank to avoid injuring this fish. It needs expert care.

The Black Bubble-eye

Another fancy species, the Black Bubble-eye is to the Bubble-eye what the Black Moor is to the Telescope— a black, velvety-covered version of the same fish. The information about the Bubble-eye applies to this fish.

This is an appropriately named fish, for it looks like an egg with fins. With a short, round, egg-shaped body, the Egg Fish lacks a dorsal fin, but has a large fantail and large pectoral and pelvic fins. This is a very popular fish in China and was a popular goldfish in the United States and England for some time. It has now fallen out of favor and is difficult to find.

It is most commonly found in a metallic-orange coloration as well as calico. A black version of this fish has also been bred, but these are extremely rare.

Meteor

This is one of the strangest and most exotic of all goldfish because it is the only one that does not have a tail. Roundish in shape like an Egg Fish, it has a high, erect dorsal fin and a large anal fin, both of which are large and long enough to make up for the missing caudal fin. Meteors are very rare. However, the peaking interest in this breed may bring them notoriety soon. It is also thought that this fish might descend from the Nymph Goldfish, being a tail-less version of that breed.

Your Happy Healthy Goldfish

Your Goldfish or fishes' Name(s) _____

Your Goldfish or fishes' Breed(s) _____
_____

Where Your Goldfish Came From _____
_____

Your Goldfish Aquarium

    Make_____

    Model _____

    Size _____

    Type of Filter_____

    Other Accessories _____

Your Goldfish or fishes' Name(s) _____

Your Goldfish's Favorite Foods _____

Your Goldfish's Health

    Name of Veterinarian _____

    Address _____

    Phone Number

    Description of Illness _____ date noticed _____

    Description of Illness _____ date noticed _____

    Description of Illness _____ date noticed _____

Your Goldfish's Breeding Record

    Date of Spawning _____

    Date of Hatching _____

    Date of First Culling/Number Culled_____

    Dates of Later Cullings/Numbers Culled _____

Your Goals for Your Goldfish Hobby _____
_____

What
Your

part two

Goldfish Needs

chapter 4

Setting Up Your
Goldfish
Aquarium

There is no more popular image of the goldfish than in a typical goldfish bowl. However, there is no more harmful place for a goldfish than this very inhumane contraption. While goldfish are extremely easy to care for, one of the things that must be guaranteed them is well-aerated water. The goldfish bowl prevents this.

The typical goldfish bowl is wide in the middle and narrow up top. What you need is an aquarium or container that gives you maximum water surface-to-air ratios. The more water surface exposed to air, the more oxygen and gas will exchange, resulting in enough air for your goldfish to breathe comfortably.

For anyone who has had a goldfish in a goldfish bowl, the one thing you will remember is the goldfish near the surface of the water, breathing rather heavily. This is because the goldfish was actually suffocating. The oxygen in the water had been quickly used up, leaving the fish no choice but to hang near the surface and gulp for air. This is not good for your fish. A muddy puddle in a deep pothole would probably be better.

Also, a Common Goldfish will grow to ten to fourteen inches in length—but not in a bowl. You generally need one gallon of water for every inch of goldfish, unless you are purposely trying to dwarf your fish. What your goldfish needs is an aquarium.

Fish Tanks

Most tanks today are made of glass and sealed with a silicone rubber cement that is both extremely strong and water-resistant. Never accept a tank that has any scratches on the glass or any spots that are not caulked with the silicone rubber cement. These tanks will have a tendency to either leak or burst.

The first thing you need to remember when placing your tank on a surface is that it will be filled with water—*and water is heavy!* Water weighs approximately 8 pounds per gallon. A 10-gallon tank weighs approximately 80 pounds and a 20-gallon tank would be approximately 160 pounds. It is important that you use the strongest piece of furniture possible, or buy one of the specially constructed aquarium stands available at your local pet or department store.

Where Do I Put the Aquarium?

When you choose an aquarium, the first thing is not to consider the size, but rather, where you are going to keep it. First choose the room, then the place within the room.

Whichever room you choose, never place the tank in front of a window. The result will be algae—and lots of it. While light is very necessary, placing the tank in front of a window will make for cleaning chores of the worst kind. Placing a tank near a window, but not in front of it, is the best of all possible locations.

What Else Do I Need to Know When I Buy a Tank?

When you buy a goldfish tank, buy an aquarium that will offer the greatest amount of surface area. Surface area refers to the part where the water meets the air. A deep 20-gallon tank will offer less surface area than a long 20-gallon tank. You don't particularly want to go deep. Generally it means that the water won't be especially well aerated and it also means that it will be difficult to adjust things and to clean the tank because many things on the bottom will be more difficult to reach. Neither are the fish interested in going too deep. Goldfish would rather swim farther than deeper.

Shape is also important because the better aerated the water, the more fish you can comfortably house. A longer tank, with more surface area, offers the hobbyist the option of supporting more fish. Maybe only one or two, but that certainly is a big value to the beginner.

Covers or Hoods?

The first things to buy for your tank are a cover and a light. The cover performs a number of functions. First, it stops unwanted objects from entering the tank and possibly injuring the fish. Second, it stops the fish from jumping out of the tank, as they sometimes want to do. This, of course, can be fatal if no one is around to find them and return them to the water—if they survive the fall. Third, the cover stops splashes from affecting the carpeting, the hardwood floor or any valuable furniture near by. Fourth, it keeps the water from damaging the light over the tank.

If the cover is made of glass (many today are made of plastic), make sure that it is not too thin. It tends to get bumped and leaned on, or may need to support heavy objects—none of which is desirable, but which happens. A cheap, thin cover made of glass will easily break. A glass cover approximately one-eighth-inch thick should be fine.

Whatever the cover, it should also provide you with easy access to the tank itself. Many are segmented in such a way that they have an area that lifts up so you don't have to remove the whole thing every time you feed your fish. Many provide for just such a situation; however, make sure that yours does when you buy it. Some covers also come with a light attached.

Surface area is an extremely important consideration when purchasing a tank. Note how much larger the surface-to-air ratio is for the tank vs. the bowl.

Lights

Lighting is necessary both for illumination and to promote plant growth. Your pet shop is usually equipped with the various lightbulbs and lamps necessary to furnish your tank with light. The light is usually enclosed in a housing that sits on top of your cover. Many lights today are fluorescent. These are cool and do not unnecessarily heat the water. They also tend to spread light more evenly and run on lower wattage than incandescent lights with tungsten filaments.

Incandescent lights offer good lighting and will give plants the amount of light they need. No matter whether you choose fluorescent or incandescent, make sure that you choose a white or natural or daylight-grade color light.

The pet shop where you buy your lighting will be able to supply you with the proper bulbs for the lighting you chose. You need to know how long your tank is so that you can calculate the wattage necessary to illuminate the tank properly. The rule is generally 2 to 2.5 watts per gallon of water. A 10-gallon tank would then require 20 to 25 watts of light from the lamp above. Again, this should be well distributed by the lamp and should extend the entire length of the tank.

Heaters

Welcome to the world of the cold-water aquarist. Because you are choosing goldfish, you do not absolutely need to have an aquarium heater. The hardier strains of goldfish, as has already been discussed, can generally withstand temperatures almost down to freezing. Some of the other varieties are less hardy, but can easily withstand temperatures in the low 60°F range, which is low enough to kill some tropical fish strains.

Provided you live in a warm climate or have heating in your home, there is normally no need for a heater in your aquarium. However, the smaller the tank, the more quickly the temperature may change. It is for this reason that many people have heaters.

Having a heater is a wise precaution. It will keep your aquarium at a constant temperature and make your life a little easier. Thermostated heaters are usually submersible, and have external controls. The thermostat can be set or reset at any time. A pilot or warning light usually lets you know that the heater is on. Never, ever pull your heater out of the water while it is on, as this is a good way to ruin your thermostat and possibly crack the tube housing the heating element.

Heaters come in different sizes, as do tanks. Just as in buying a light, you must buy a heater that is right for your tank. And just like lights, you buy heaters by wattage. The average rule is 5 watts for every gallon of water. A ten-gallon tank, then, requires a 50-watt heater, a twenty-gallon tank requires a 100-watt heater, a thirty-gallon tank calls for a 150-watt heater, etc.

Some people think that with larger aquariums you should split the wattage in half between two heaters, one at either end of a tank. On a thirty-gallon tank, then, you would have two 75-watt heaters.

There are three basic types of heaters. There is the classic submerged heater, which attaches to one corner and has external controls. There are also undertank or dry heaters, essentially heating pads that fit under the tank. And finally there are completely submersible heaters, which are mountable with included suction cups or other types of brackets.

A heater should be placed where it will come into contact with the circulating water, so that it will warm the water effectively and maintain temperatures consistently.

Examples of thermometers: (1) A digital thermometer that attaches on the outside of the aquarium. (2) A metal thermometer; this type attaches to the side of the aquarium and hangs in the water.

Thermometers

You need a thermometer to monitor the temperature of the water. There are two types of thermometers that are popular. The first is the internal floating thermometer. The second is the external stick-on thermometer. The external thermometers tend to read a bit low—probably 2°F—so keep that in mind.

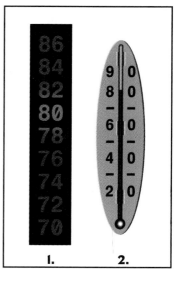

Filters

There are three basic types of filters: box filters, which go inside the tank; power filters, which go outside the tank; and undergravel filters. The first two have a series of layers of wadding and charcoal to remove debris and chemicals from the water, while the undergravel filter uses the gravel and creates a natural filter.

Let's discuss first what the filter does. The filter has two or three ostensible purposes, depending on what kind you use. First, it cleanses and purifies the water. Second, it circulates the water. Third, in most cases, it aerates the water.

I would recommend a power filter for most beginner aquariums. They are easy to clean and change, and they clean more water faster than any of the other filters. This is important with goldfish, as goldfish are not the neatest of fish. A strong filter is needed to take care of them.

If your tank is on the scale of ten gallons or larger and you want goldfish, use a power filter. Goldfish are too messy and too active for a box filter, which will not provide enough air, or an undergravel filter, which will not be strong enough to sift out all the debris—which goldfish seem to create in an endless supply.

BOX FILTER

Known also as an inside, corner or bottom filter, the box filter is the most standard of all filters. It's usually shaped like a cube and is packed with a small layer of fibrous material, then a layer of charcoal, then more fibrous material on top. This staple or mat (as it is sometimes called) should be tamped down, but not too tightly packed. The materials should be loose enough for water to get through easily.

The first or uppermost layer of fibrous material sifts out any large debris. This is sometimes referred to as mechanical filtration. The second layer, the charcoal, purifies the water chemically, taking out any toxic materials as well. It also makes the water crystal clear. (The same filtration system is used in many home water filtration units.) The third or bottommost layer is for sifting out any other debris before the water is pumped back out via a tube with air rushing out.

The air comes from a tube which is attached to the top of the filter leading out of the tank. This is attached to an air pump. As the air races through the filter, that water is pushed out, drawing in more water through small slits on the top of the filter.

The air pump is outside the tank and must be plugged into a wall socket. Finding a quiet, powerful and small pump is important with any filtration device which depends on one of these. The more powerful the air pump, the more powerful the filter and the more aerated the water.

This Telescope-eyed fish is healthy thanks to the proper care of its aquarium.

During the entire process, biological filtration is taking place, rather than mechanical or chemical filtration. As water passes through, some toxic products are converted into nitrates used by plants, and some dissipate into the air.

OUTSIDE OR POWER FILTERS

These filters hang on the outside of the tank, usually in the back of the tank so as not to interfere with the view. Usually they are powered by their own motor; however, there are some that will use an air pump to power them. The filter operates on the same premise as the previous one. Water passes from the tank through an upside-down U-shaped tube into the filter. There

61

it goes through the same series of wadded media as in the box filter before it is pumped back out into the tank.

These are among the most powerful filters available. They are not better in terms of filtration media, because they use the same materials. They are better because these types of filters tend to move more water faster.

UNDERGRAVEL FILTERS

Biologically speaking, the undergravel filter is the best. Placed in the tank before anything else, it is a plastic plate with tiny slits throughout that covers the bottom of the tank. Gravel, plants, and so on are placed on top of this. Air is pumped to the bottom of the filter, where it then goes back up a tube, forcing water, which is allowed entry, up the tube. This creates a suction, drawing water from underneath the gravel. This filter uses the gravel as a filtering medium.

After a while, aerobic bacteria congregate. These bacteria form the core of the filter, consuming or dissolving all types of matter in the water flowing through the filter. It takes some time for the bacteria population to develop. It may take anywhere from one to two months before the bacteria population is large enough to make a difference.

> **WHAT IF I MUST USE A FISHBOWL?**
>
> If you must use a bowl, make sure that you select one of the smallest possible goldfish and choose the largest possible bowl. One beneficial item available for bowls is an undergravel/bottom filter. The bases of these types of filters are round in shape and because of the air used to operate them, the water will be better aerated. However, it really is important, if you can, to get the biggest bowl possible, and to make sure it offers as great a surface area as possible.

Uneaten food, feces and other substances natural to aquarium life decay and become ammonium compounds, which are not good for fish. As water passes through the gravel, the aerobic bacteria convert the ammonium compounds into nitrites and then into nitrates. The fish can live with nitrates.

For goldfish, it is important to place enough gravel in the tank so that the fish do not dig so deep into the gravel that they disturb the bacterial population you are trying so hard to establish. Since goldfish are such good bottom feeders and gravel movers, they sometimes make this type of filtration difficult.

If you have live plants, this system is both a blessing and a curse. The nitrates produced by the bacteria are great for your plants and will cause them to thrive. However, because of the way the undergravel filter works, the filtering process wreaks havoc on the plants' root systems, ruining their chances of survival. There are two solutions to this. You can terrace the gravel in one area and place most of the plants there. In the terraced area your plants will meet with less turbulence from the filtering system. Or you can buy a plate that is small enough to leave one area open on the aquarium floor so that you can place the plants there without too much disturbance. Or you can try a combination of these.

Air Pumps

Depending on what kind of filter you decide to use, you can then decide what size air pump you need. If you choose an outside or power filter, you need only a small pump to use for an airstone or other device to supply more oxygen to the water.

If you choose a box or an undergravel filter, you will want a more powerful pump so you can easily operate those devices as well as an airstone. Air pumps are left on 24 hours a day. They are never shut off except when you are dismantling the filters or the tank for cleaning. The cost of running an air pump 24 hours a day is negligible.

There are two basic kinds of pumps: diaphragm pumps, which have a vibrating rubber diaphragm, and piston pumps. Both are solid additions to any aquarium; however, while the diaphragm types require no attention, piston pumps do require oiling occasionally. Piston pumps tend to deliver more power, though. Air pumps may generate some noise, so quietness is a special sales feature aside from strength, when choosing the right one for you. Pumps are made to support anything from a large bowl to a slew of tanks. Talk to your pet professional regarding your specific tank.

Aeration

Goldfish need a lot of oxygen in the water. The more oxygen in the tank, the more goldfish you will be able to house comfortably, within reason. Having an airstone or some other air-release device can generally raise the number of fish you can support by about two for a 10-gallon tank, three for a 20-gallon tank and four for a 30-gallon tank.

You will use your fishnet frequently.

Airstones are generally made of porous rock attached at the end of an air hose. The stone gives off tiny bubbles, which aerate the water. You don't want too fine a mist—tiny bubbles are best. Other air releasers are usually made of plastic and are weighted at the bottom. They come as sunken treasure chests, fallen barrels, old-fashioned underwater divers—there's an amazing assortment to choose from. Remember, you don't want big bubbles racing to the surface. You want a steady stream of medium-sized bubbles that take their time going upward, giving them a chance to add oxygen to the water.

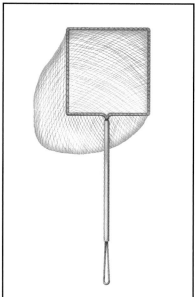

These are very important features of any aquarium setup, and I strongly recommend that you have at least one in a 10- or 20-gallon tank, and at least two in a 30-gallon tank or larger.

Other Accessories

There are any number of accessories available for aquariums. Listed below are some of the more important ones.

Air Hoses   Sold at pet stores, this plastic tubing will enable you to attach your air pump to the filter and/or aeration devices. Air hoses should snugly fit all joints and no air should escape anywhere. If there is air leakage, the resultant loss of pressure more often than not will cause the filter not to live up to its potential or possibly cause your air pump to burn out faster.

Air Valves   Air valves enable the aquarist to run additional aeration or filter devices off a single pump. A single pump should be able to supply a filter and an aeration device. An air valve takes the feed from the air pump and then distributes it to two, three, four or more valves which can be used or shut off in case of non-use. This allows you to send pumped air to different devices in different parts of the tank. It also allows you to control the air flow to these different places.

Algae Sponge or Aquarium Cleaner   This is a sponge that is usually attached to a long handle and is used for scraping down the inside of the tank without having to empty it out. This can be done while the fish are still in the tank. It is good for removing algae which has grown on the inside walls of the tank. The sponge is strong enough to scrape off algae but will not scratch the glass.

Aquarium Screens or Backgrounds   Aquarium screens are placed on the outside of the tank, facing the front of the tank. The idea is to hide the tubing, filters, pumps, etc., that are usually kept at the back of the aquarium. Aquaria most often are placed against a wall. Aquarium screens prevent you from seeing the wallpaper or paint on the wall behind the tank, since many times these wall colorings are not especially a part of the natural habitat of goldfish.

Fishnet   This is an important piece of equipment. The fishnet should not be too small (leaving you too small an area with which to catch your fish) or too big (making it difficult to maneuver inside your tank and around the various rocks, plants, etc.). You will use this more than you think. You will need it when you have to take out an ailing or dead fish, or an aggressive fish, and when you need to take out all the fish to clean the aquarium.

Vacuums   There are such things as aquarium vacuums. These are usually small hand-pump siphons that extract larger debris from the aquarium floor. Especially with goldfish, these are quite handy. They perform a very necessary task in helping to clean your tank and maintain a debris-free environment.

Aquascaping

In general, aquascaping means setting up the inside of the tank so that it is pleasing to the human eye

as well as pleasing to the fish. Aquascaping includes the placement of rocks, air releases, plants, and any wood pieces you've decided to include. The concept is to set up something resembling a natural habitat. I will discuss whether to have real rocks, wood, or plants instead of fake ones later in the book. Let me deal with the layout now; you can decide later if it will be filled with living materials or artificial decorations.

Think about how you'd like your aquarium to look before you start aquascaping. This fish is by a swordplant.

Where you have placed your aquarium will dictate how you should aquascape it. If it can only be viewed from the front, then you should plan to aquascape for a frontal view. However, if the aquarium can be approached from many different angles, then those angles need to be addressed as well.

Some people make a rough sketch of what they would like, or find a photograph of what they would like to do. It is advisable to have a solid idea of what you want before you go into the store. By understanding what you want, you can plan better when it comes to terracing your gravel, and placing large stones or logs which will hide tubing and filters, etc. Depending on the plants you choose, some will need to be bunched together while others will need to be alone. Most aquarists tend to place their taller plants toward the back of the tank. If you want an aquarium screen, this should also be taken into account when deciding on your aquascaping.

As far as plants go, never have even numbers, as that symmetry in nature mostly does not exist. Place the smaller plants and objects up front. Also, land rocks are not as good as rocks taken from ponds. Land rocks tend to be jagged and could injure your fish. Rocks found in streams and ponds tend to be rounded and are better for fish. Of all rocks, shale and slate tend to be the best. Driftwood is a nice touch, but make sure to have driftwood that is weighted down. It is best to buy this from a pet store, so that it is guaranteed to be properly cured for your goldfish.

Don't place too many objects in the tank—don't overaquascape. Make sure to leave an area open for swimming. This is generally called the swimming space. Fish like to have a place to hide, especially in the plants you have supplied, but they need a place to swim and exert themselves as well. It is usually best if this is left open up front, so that you can view the fish when they are most active.

It is true of rocks and wood that these are best when purchased through pet stores, so as to avoid any problems of toxic properties that might contaminate the water and fish. If you must use rocks from around your home, it is a good idea to steam-clean them first. *Never place seashells or any marine or sea life in with your goldfish. These are not fresh-water items and will cause the water to become much too alkaline for your fish.*

IF YOUR GOLDFISH GETS GRAVEL STUCK IN ITS MOUTH

Goldfish sometimes get bits of gravel caught in their mouths. Usually this will dislodge itself over a matter of several hours without damage to the fish. However, in those cases where the gravel does not dislodge, attempt the following, recommended by the Goldfish Society of America in its *Official Guide to the Goldfish:*

1. Capture the fish with a fishnet.

2. Hold the fish head down and press against both sides of the lips, opening the mouth.

3. With your other hand, press the throat behind the stone. Relief is usually immediate.

Gravel

Gravel is an important consideration in setting up any fish tank, but especially so with goldfish. Goldfish are excellent scavengers and bottom feeders. They will take up big bunches of gravel, hold them in their mouths and then spit them back out. Goldfish are also known for moving gravel around quite a bit, which sometimes makes aquascaping difficult.

The gravel should be no smaller or finer than medium coarse so that it is not accidently ingested, and it should be smooth so that it does not damage the fishes' mouths.

Setting Up Your Aquarium

Follow these steps to set up your aquarium.

1. In a separate container, wash the gravel. Do not use soap of any kind. Empty the gravel into a container, fill it up with water, and then dump the water and start all over again. You must agitate the gravel during each rinse by moving the gravel around while submerged to get the dirt and other toxic debris off the gravel. Generally, for brand-new gravel, four or five thorough rinsings are enough. Don't skimp on this step, as uncleaned gravel will not only make for cloudy water, but water unsafe for your goldfish.

2. Make sure the tank is exactly where you want it to be. You should not move the tank once you begin to fill it. (Tanks are not made for movement once they have been filled.) Pour the gravel gently into the tank and begin the aquascaping of your tank. Terrace the gravel so that the gravel is as high as it goes toward the back of the tank.

3. Add any large pieces now—rocks, pieces of wood, etc. All these should be thoroughly rinsed off before being put into the tank. Again, don't use soap in cleaning anything—just clear water.

4. If you have an airstone or air release, put it in place now.

5. Add the water to the tank. Use tap water. The container to carry water from the tap to the aquarium should be free of any soap or other element that would dirty the water. It is best, if you have a large piece in the tank, to pour the water on it, trying not to disturb your aquascape too much. After water is added, you may need to re-aquascape.

6. Place the filter and heater in the tank and position them.

7. Place the plants. If you are using live plants, remember to weight them down. Place the thermometer in now as well.

8. Plug it all in after you have set it up and hooked up all the hoses. Turn it on. Make sure the heater is properly adjusted and that the filter is working.

Note: Don't place the fish in the tank immediately. Wait at least forty-eight hours before placing fish in this environment. The water needs to distill for twenty-four hours and you want to make sure the tank is running properly before putting in the fish. Some experts would have you wait as long as two weeks, but I think that's too long for any enthusiastic hobbyist. Keep in mind that goldfish are a fairly hardy species.

The Water

Goldfish are freshwater, cold-water fish. As long as you have let the water stand forty-eight hours or so before putting the goldfish in the aquarium, everything should be fine. Goldfish, even the exotics, tend to be hardy where water is concerned. However, it is important to be able to control the water, because there are a number of things that influence fish where water is concerned.

There are two water-quality parameters a goldfish enthusiast should continually watch: hard as opposed to soft water and acidity versus alkalinity. Before you place your goldfish in the aquarium make sure to test the water for both.

Hardness Hardness refers to the amount of salts, namely calcium and magnesium, in the water. Water that lacks salts is referred to as soft. Hardness can be dealt with in a number of ways. While goldfish can survive generally hard water, there is no need to place your fish at risk. A water-hardness test and correction kits can be purchased at your local pet store.

*The Nitrogen
Cycle.*

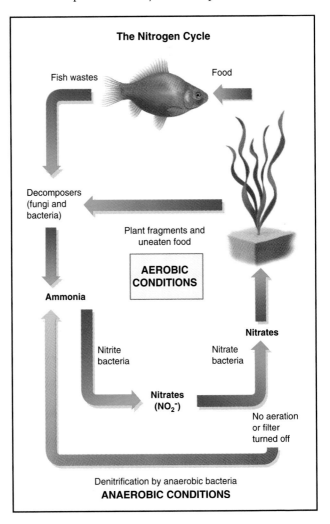

The Nitrogen Cycle

Food

Fish wastes

Decomposers
(fungi and
bacteria)

Plant fragments and
uneaten food

**AEROBIC
CONDITIONS**

Ammonia

Nitrates

Nitrite
bacteria

Nitrate
bacteria

**Nitrates
(NO_2^-)**

No aeration
or filter
turned off

Denitrification by anaerobic bacteria
ANAEROBIC CONDITIONS

pH pH refers to the amount of acidity in the water. Neutral water has a pH of 7. Acidic water has a pH less than 7 and akaline water has a pH greater than 7: The more acidic, the lower the pH, and the more akaline, the higher the pH. Goldfish hobbyists should maintain their aquarium's pH somewhere between 6.5 and 8.5. This can be determined by using a pH test kit, which can be purchased at all pet shops.

Nitrates   Another problem in goldfish tanks is that of the nitrate cycle. Fish wastes, uneaten foods and plant fragments decay and break down into ammonium compounds. Ammonia is not good for your fish. Natural bacteria that grow in the aquarium convert these ammonium compounds into nitrites. Nitrites are not good for your goldfish either, although they are less harmful than ammonia. A second type of bacteria which also grow naturally in all aquaria turn these nitrites into nitrates. Goldfish can withstand great amounts of nitrates without too many problems. Plants, however, use nitrates and give off oxygen in return.

> ### BRINGING YOUR GOLDFISH HOME
>
> When you bring home your goldfish, your pet dealer will have put the fish in clear plastic baggies filled with water and enough oxygen for a short trip. Ask to have this plastic bag placed in another bag—a paperbag or a dark opaque plastic bag, if possible. The first thing you must do is resist the temptation to take the fish out in the light and gawk at it. Bringing the fish from the dark into the light and then back to dark will put the fish into shock. This weakens the fish and its resistance to other possible maladies. Keep it in the bag until you get home.

Since all of this happens naturally, you might think that there's nothing to worry about. Wrong! In new aquariums many beginners experience "new tank syndrome." New tank syndrome is when all your new fish die from shock. Don't fall victim to this. The bacteria populations that build in your tank can take anywhere from two to four months to establish themselves, depending on certain conditions. Nitrate test kits are available and are invaluable when starting up a new aquarium.

Placing the Fish in the Tank

It is important to follow the steps described below. While goldfish are a hardy breed, they are not the best travelers, and tend to go into shock during transportation and introduction into a new tank.

1. When you get home, take the plastic baggies of fish and place them in the tank without opening

them. This helps to allow the temperature in the bag to acclimate to the temperature of the tank. Let it sit for ten or fifteen minutes.

2. Open the bag and let air get in it. Take a handful of water from the tank and pour it into the bag. Let this stand for another ten or fifteen minutes.

3. Lift the bag out of the aquarium and discard half to two thirds of the water in the bag (you don't want to dump a lot of water from someone else's aquarium into your own). Place a fishnet in front of the bag just to make sure the fish don't accidently swim out. Pour some more water from your aquarium into the bag and let it sit for another five to ten minutes.

4. Dump the remaining contents of the bag into your tank, fish and all.

Note: It is important to know that you really should buy and introduce into the aquarium all your goldfish within three to six weeks of each other. Introducing a new goldfish much later, after the fish have already set up certain patterns, may result in aggressive behavior, disrupting the tank. All the fish should be of approximately the same size and age.

Plants—
Living or
Artificial?

The one thing goldfish fanciers all know, though some would not like to admit it, is that goldfish are not especially kind to live plants. In most cases, goldfish treat plants the way we do potato chips—they munch on 'em. This is the best argument against live plants and for artificial ones.

Many experienced goldfish hobbyists know that to keep live plants in with goldfish requires ultimately more care for the plants than for the fish them-

This goldfish is in front of a Java Fern.

selves. It can be done, but it requires work and constant attention. You should consider how much time you want to devote to your fish tank before you decide on artificial or live plants. There are many goldfish experts who do not keep goldfish with either gravel or plants, but that's not aesthetically pleasing.

Another positive about artificial plants is that there are a great number to choose from, and many of the better-made ones look like the real thing. As with anything in life, the cheaper the artificial plants you buy, the more plastic they look. Most of the better artificial plant manufacturers provide replicas of all the plants described in this chapter.

Why Live Plants?

First of all, live plants are an excellent source of oxygen as a result of photosynthesis. Plants absorb the nitrates that naturally occur in your fish tank and might become a serious problem if there is too much buildup. They provide shade and hiding, egg-laying sites, and yes, even if handled properly, provide food for your goldfish. Some experienced goldfish keepers plant two different types of plants in their aquariums: the tough plants that cannot be so easily eaten by goldfish and smaller, more tender plants that are stocked purposely to be eaten. The latter group is provided so that the former group might grow more successfully.

Plant Types

There are three major types of plants: rooted, bunches and floaters. *Rooted* plants usually grow in numbers, but separate from one another. *Bunches* are plants that quickly reproduce off one stem, and can quickly envelop a tank. *Floaters* are floating plants whose root system dangles in the water. These usually grow near the surface, or in some cases, right out of the water. Each of these groups will provide two or three varieties that can survive goldfish.

If you choose live plants, please follow this advice. Pick no more than two or three types of plant—two is preferable. Pay attention to these sets of plants and learn how to deal with them as best you can. The simpler you keep it, the faster and better you will learn to grow and keep plants. I would suggest *Sagittaria* (arrowhead) and *elodea* (pondweed). Both are hardy and hard to kill. Don't feel bad or give up if you kill the first set of plants—eventually you'll master this difficult phase of aquarium maintenance. I would recommend planting them to the back and sides of the tank, because if you are good and lucky, they will grow large and might obscure your vision should you plant them up front.

Plastic or Real?

Personally, while I think the benefits of live plants are great and eventually must be mastered by anyone wanting to be a long-term hobbyist, the beginner should use artificial plants. For the beginner, understanding how an aquarium works and the attention needed to run it successfully need to be learned before becoming a freshwater botanist. There is nothing worse than having to scoop up the brown remains of what used to

Live plants are an excellent source of oxygen.

be plant life in your new aquarium. It is better to learn how your fish react to so many different disturbances and how to deal with the many other issues of aquarium maintenance before learning how to grow plants successfully and how to defend them from your goldfish.

Regardless of whether you choose live or artificial plants, I think the following recommendations and guidelines should be of interest to anyone reading this book. Even if you choose the artificial plant route, you will need to know which plants you should consider purchasing to simulate a natural habitat for your goldfish. Remember, there is no shame in using artificial plants.

Rooted Plants

There are three types of rooted plants that you should plant with goldfish: *Sagittaria, Vallisneria* and Amazon sword plants. These do not appeal to goldfish as much as other plants might. But make no mistake, goldfish will eventually, if they have a mind to, destroy almost any plant.

Sagittaria and *Vallisneria* are both stolon-type plants. That is, they reproduce by sending out a runner, which eventually, given enough time, will grow into another plant. Wait until these new plants have developed a root system before separating them and planting them where you want. Or you may weigh down the new plant where you want it instead of cutting it. In this case, the plant will eventually separate itself.

These plants should be pruned whenever there is brown found on any part of them. Decay on most freshwater aquatic plants must be clipped off immediately, before it kills the plant itself.

Sagittaria (Arrowhead) These plants can grow up to thirty-six inches in height. With long, straight leaves, they are best when placed in bunches. They are generally sturdy plants. For reproduction, you must cut runners from the stolon and then plant them. Or you can weigh down the new plant where you want to, while it is still attached to the parent, and it will separate on its own accord. These plants can survive in temperatures as high as 77°F, but they are also hardy cold-water plants and do not require a lot of light to thrive.

Vallisneria spiralis Again, these are pretty hardy plants. *Vallisneria* has long, ribbonlike leaves that spiral upward. It looks like a curly version of *Sagittaria* and will grow approximately two feet long. For reproduction, you must either cut the runner from the stolon and then plant it, or weigh down the new plant while it is still attached to the parent. These plants are not quite as hardy as *Sagittaria,* as they have a more delicate temperature zone ranging from 59°F to 72°F.

Echinodorus brevipedicellatus (Amazon Sword Plant)

More popularly known as the Amazon Sword Plant, Echinodorus may have as many as thirty to forty leaves growing from it. The leaves are broad in the middle and tapered at each end. There is also a broad-leafed Amazon sword plant. This plant does well in medium to strong sunlight, or, alternatively, it should get approximately eight to ten hours of electric light a day. It can survive in temperatures up to 80°F. Reproduction is similar to the previous two types mentioned.

This fish is in front of the Vallisneria spiralis, a rooted plant.

Bunched Plants

Again, given my predisposition to goldfish and their tendencies, I will mention only a few of the bunched plants that I feel will be more than satisfactory in this type of environment. Elodea and milfoil are similar enough, however, offering the aquarist more than enough choice to make the aquascape interesting and healthy.

These are plants that propagate by way of cuttings. You buy cuttings from your pet dealer. Slice off the bottom inch and, on the next inch, take off many of the leaves. Weigh down the bunch and plant the plucked inch into the gravel. These plants will take hold quickly and grow just as fast. Don't buy any plant that is already browning, as it will shortly be dead. Buy only solidly green specimens.

Anacharis canadensis (Pondweed)

Also known as elodea or pondweed, this is a favorite for cold freshwater tanks. Pondweed is long, with narrow stalks that sprout rings of thick green leaves. In a regular tank these plants would need constant pruning. That may or may not be the case in your goldfish tank. However, they grow fast and can sometimes outgrow even a school of goldfishes' hunger.

Elodea is reproduced by cutting off the lower inch when you buy it from your pet store and planting the remainder firmly in the gravel. They should be weighted. Generally speaking, they usually root pretty quickly and are very hardy. They can withstand temperatures up to approximately 80°F.

Myriophyllum spicatum (Foxtail) Also known as milfoil or foxtail, this is another favorite in freshwater tanks. Given strong light, Milfoil can sometimes grow three to four inches in a week's time. They look much like elodea, except that they sprout much finer leaves, like eyelashes, in rings around the stalk. Otherwise, much of what goes for elodea also holds true for milfoil.

Floating Plants

Floating plants are highly recommended for goldfish but, unfortunately, for outdoor ponds only. These plants require great amounts of strong sunlight and generally grow much too large for aquarium use.

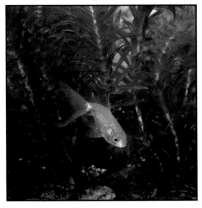

An example of the plant Anacharis.

While they have been grown and maintained by experts, it is not recommended even for journeymen aquarists. If your heart is set on floating plants, however, the three recommended are water hyacinth, duckweed and *Riccia* (crystalwort).

Eichhornia crassipes (Water Hyacinth) Also known as the water hyacinth, this lusty plant is found all over the United States. It grows so quickly that it has been known to make waterways impassable. These plants provide great shading for the fish and make the water both oxygen and nutrient rich. This is one of the best plants for goldfish, as the root system is also ideal for egg laying. When the flowers bloom, they may grow as high as twelve inches. The flowers of water hyacinths grown indoors last for less than twenty-four hours.

Lemna minor (Duckweed)   Also known as duckweed, this plant floats on top of the water in no fewer than two egg-shaped leaves at a time. They have a sigle root. These are much more delicate plants than water hyacinths, but are certainly hardy. They propagate quickly. Like water hyacinths or water lilies, duckweed will quickly cover a small pond. It needs lots of light and will respond in kind.

Riccia   Also known as crystalwort, this is an ideal plant for goldfish. It can be used for egg laying, for nourishment and for shade. Its root system is softer than the hyacinth's, and allows for various uses by adult goldfish as well as their small fry. *Riccia* needs a minimum of six hours of light a day. Their only danger is that they do tend to have parasites. When you buy them, make sure that you have only the healthiest-looking specimens.

Foxtail is an aquarium favorite.

6

Feeding
Your
Goldfish

Basic Feeding

Goldfish can survive for a lifetime on flake foods. However, it must be stressed that if you want active, colorful, healthy fish, you must vary their diets. If you are interested in breeding your goldfish at all, it probably will not be worth it if you're not interested in investing the necessary amount of time in their diets. Goldfish will grow bored with flake food as their only source of nutrition. You can use it as their staple food, but you really should make an attempt to substitute other foods several times a week to ensure the best possible results.

One of the reasons for varying the food intake of goldfish is to ensure that they have a balanced diet. The foods given goldfish should supply them with the same essentials that all vertebrates need. **Proteins, vitamins** and **minerals** are obviously important for bones, etc. However, they are also important when considering Lionheads, Orandas and Pompons especially, or any other kind of goldfish that has some kind of headgrowth. **Fats** and **carbohydrates** are, of course, necessary for energy. Fat storage is important for fish that live outdoors so that they can sustain themselves through the winter months. **Fiber** provides the diet with bulk, and is important for a healthy digestive system. Goldfish should get something from the vegetable, cereal and fish or meat food groups in equal amounts.

What Do I Feed My Goldfish?

There are as many different types of food for your goldfish as there are different types of goldfish. There is, of course, flake food. Flake foods in general supply goldfish with a very balanced diet. These foods are well designed to provide goldfish with the essentials necessary for a long and happy life.

However, there are other types of food. Omnivore is a very good classification for goldfish, because they will eat everything. They will eat red worms, white worms, earthworms, tubifex. They will eat brine shrimp, mosquito larvae and fruit flies. They love almost any kind of seafood—crab, lobster, oysters, clams—either fresh or canned. They can also be fed canned foods, such as canned vegetables—beans are especially good for them. Fresh spinach, broccoli and cauliflower are also excellent additions.

FOOD CATEGORIES

The following is a breakdown, food by food, of what you might feed your fish. There are basically four different food categories: flake or dried foods; frozen or freeze-dried foods; live foods; and table scraps or household foods. Of these, the most dangerous are live foods. Except for earthworms, most of these have an excellent chance of carrying diseases which may infect or even kill your fish. Frozen or freeze-dried foods are really the hobbyist's best friend. They are an excellent source of protein and goldfish love them. More importantly, they offer all the benefits of live foods, but don't suffer the possibility of carrying diseases or causing infection. Table scraps or household foods are also an excellent source of nutrition.

FLAKES OR DRIED FOODS

There are numerous manufacturers of flake or dried foods, and these foods are available in a wide variety of shapes and sizes. The most important thing to know is that goldfish do not have the same nutritional needs as tropical fish. Their body makeup and composition are substantially different from tropicals, despite their both being fish. Consequently, fish food manufacturers produce flake and dried foods especially for goldfish, which address their unique requirements.

Many dried food manufacturers have begun marketing feeding kits that promise to improve growth and color. The results are mixed, but one thing is for sure. Don't buy these kits unless they are exclusively aimed at goldfish. If a particular type of food is aimed at tropical fish in general, it is probably not a good buy for goldfish. Goldfishes' nutritional needs differ greatly from community or incompatible tropical fish, and the results will almost surely not be there.

Dried foods can be prepared in a number of ways, including flakes, or compressed into pellets, also known as granules (which are bite-size chunks), or tablets (the largest of the consumable compressed dried foods). Some manufacturers make vitamin-enriched flake food. Breeders tend to dislike them because the vitamins break down faster this way. Feeding the diets recommended in this book should give your goldfish its nutritional needs so supplementing isn't necessary.

LIVE FOODS

Given the best of all possible scenarios, live food is easily the best food to give your always-hungry goldfish. The problem is that in real life these foods stand the chance of being laden with disease.

Although a great many experts actually cultivate their own live food, I strongly recommend against it for beginners and hobbyists. Live foods can easily be obtained in small quantities from your local pet store and can usually be bought in one- or two-serving sizes. The live food you get at your local pet store is to a great degree safe, since the store owner is probably feeding some of it to his own fish as well.

To ensure healthy fish, choose flake or dried foods that are specially formulated for goldfish, not for tropical fish.

The only two live foods that generally do not run the risk of carrying a disease are earthworms and brine shrimp. Both brine shrimp and earthworms are easily gotten and are an excellent addition to your fishes' diet.

Note: No matter what any expert tells you, never go searching in lakes or ponds for live foods. Since most of these are larvae, they tend to be in murky, stagnant waters. This is where they will most likely pick up parasites and other diseases which can be passed along to your fish. Unless you are a trained botanist, do not do this.

Brine Shrimp   The brine shrimp in your local pet shop probably came from the Great Salt Lake area. They are one of the best food sources available for fish of any type. And of all the live food available, these are the safest, because they do not carry diseases and are extremely safe and easy to care for. And goldfish love them!

If you want, they can also be raised from a culture. Here are the steps to follow if you wish to raise brine shrimp from a culture:

1. In a plastic or glass container, add twelve ounces of salt per gallon of water.

2. At the bottom of the container, place an operating aerator and place a stone on top of it so that it doesn't move.

3. Add two ounces of Epsom salts and one ounce of sodium bicarbonate to the container (per gallon of water).

4. Empty the container of brine eggs into the mixture. They are small and fine and should be handled with care.

5. Given a temperature of around 75°F, you should have brine shrimp in two days. You can continue to feed the shrimp brewer's yeast to keep them going until the culture is finished.

Earthworms   Earthworms are rich in protein and are an interesting dietary change for your goldfish. They are particularly valuable to hobbyists and prized by goldfish during or preceding breeding season. They are also easily obtained. You can either search for them after showers in lawns and around ponds and lakes, or you can cultivate them in your back yard. This is the only live food I recommend that a hobbyist cultivate.

Earthworms can be cultivated by taking a small patch of dirt, maybe a yard or two yards square, and throwing burlap sacks over the raw, tilled soil. Then, taking the garden hose, water the burlap sacks until they are good and wet. Do this every morning of the week. On the seventh day, lift up the burlap sacks, and Bingo, worm city! I don't recommend that you take too many to feed your fish right away, nor do I recommend that you harvest them more than once a week. The best time to harvest is usually early in the morning, before the dew has evaporated.

After you get them, rinse them off and put them in a jar with holes in the lid, and let them sit for a day or two in some dark shaded area. Rinse them each day so that they will rid their bodies of any earth they have inside of them. Rinse them off again and cut them into small bits. If you have small goldfish, say, less than four inches long, you really should dice them up. If you have goldfish that are, say, between four and six inches long, depending on their size, cut the worms into halves or thirds. Any goldfish over six inches long will be more than happy to swallow the worms whole.

Note: Make sure no herbicides or weed killers have been used in the area where you are collecting your worms. These pesticides will poison your fish.

Tubifex These long, thin, red worms, also known as sludgeworms, are not very pretty, but can be bought at the local pet store, where their chance of carrying disease is low. Like all live food, they are an excellent food source and will be gratefully appreciated by your fish.

Before feeding them to your fish, you must rinse them thoroughly in gently running water for at least one hour; if you can, do it for two more hours. Tubifex require a lot of work and are considered so risky that I advise you to feed them to your goldfish only once or twice a month. While it is possible to breed these in a culture at your home, it's very difficult and is probably not worth the risk.

Whiteworms Also known as microworms, these worms are white or beige. They can be bought in small single-serving amounts from your local pet shop. But they are also available in cultures.

HOUSEHOLD FOODS FOR YOUR FISH

Frozen (serve thawed): clams, mussels, shrimp, fish, lobster, crabmeat, oysters

Canned: the same as frozen, plus beans and peas

Raw: the same as frozen, plus ground beef, spinach, lettuce

Cooked (baked, steamed, boiled): potato, beans, peas, egg yolk, broccoli, cauliflower, breadcrumbs

While live foods and foods other than flakes are highly desirable, it is important to know that no one group supplies everything your goldfish needs. Always selecting food from one group or another will lead to overload. Too many live foods and your goldfish may not have enough fats or carbohydrates in their diet. Too much of any one food may cause digestive problems too difficult to remedy.

If you wish to raise your own culture, follow these steps:

1. In a large tray or small shallow tub, place earth and mulched leaves.

2. Water the earth and place the worms on the dirt. Also sprinkle breadcrumbs or place slices of bread on the dirt. Some authorities recommend oatmeal.

3. Place a sheet of glass over the tub and cover the tub with a sheet or blanket. Make sure the glass is touching every part of the container.

4. Place the tub in a damp place at room temperature and leave it alone for two to three weeks. Temperatures will make the maturing time vary.

5. When you unwrap the tub, the glass plate will be covered by white worms on the underside of the glass. Scrape them off and presto, a feast fit for a goldfish!

These cultures only last for approximately six weeks. If you suspect that the culture has gone bad, it is important that you dispose of the entire batch and keep none of the worms.

Daphnia　　Also known as water flea larvae, these are an excellent food for your goldfish. However, goldfish should be fed this type of food in moderation, since too much of this type of food may act as a laxative and cause serious digestive problems in your fish. Moderation is the key to everything. Daphnia are easily gotten from your local pet shop in small quantities, or it is also possible to culture them at home:

1. Fill a jar with an inch of topsoil. Tamp it down, but don't pack it hard. Some experts like to include manure, and some like to include baker's yeast as well.

2. Carefully pour in some water. Fill the jar until it is three quarters full.

3. Place the jar in the sun for a week. Wait for a good growth of algae. If there is not a good amount of algae, wait another week.

4. Add the Daphnia culture and wait ten to fourteen days.

And there you go, Daphnia! Never take more than one fifth of the culture, as this may keep the culture from recovering. You must feed the culture, and remember to continue to add brewer's yeast or manure during that time, several times a week. This culture will only last two to three weeks, but will provide at least two to three feedings a week for your goldfish.

Drosophila   These are the larvae of *Drosophila,* the wingless (actually, vestigial-winged) fruit fly, so they won't try to fly away on you. They provide your fish with a tasty treat and an excellent food source. You can sometimes buy them at the local pet store, or you can culture them at home.

If you wish to create a culture, follow these steps:

1. To water that you have boiled, add agar and some mashed banana.

2. Let the mixture stand for a few days to allow it to jell.

3. Add some fruit flies, let them sit for two weeks and you'll have Drosophila galore.

Bloodworms   Also known as two-winged fly larvae, these are usually in good supply year round and can be purchased at your local pet store. They are very difficult to cultivate at home. Because they are difficult to culture, they are usually commercially bred and therefore offer less risk to the hobbyist. Again, these can be bought in small quantities for single or double servings.

Frozen or Freeze-dried Foods

Frozen or freeze-dried foods offer the best of the live world without any of the hassles of growing a culture. They also offer the protection of being disease free. Foods included are brine shrimp, krill (shrimp a little larger than brine), tubifex worms, mosquito larvae, daphnia, and bloodworms. These are a great convenience to the hobbyist who wants to provide variety to his or her fish without having to deal with too much mess.

TABLE OR HOUSEHOLD FOODS

Table or household foods offer nutritional value and great variety to the goldfish diet. You can offer your goldfish fresh, frozen or canned oysters, clams, mussels, crabmeat, lobster, or bits of raw fish—but no canned tuna fish. Baked or boiled beans, steamed cauliflower or broccoli and boiled or baked potato are all excellent additions as well. Fresh lettuce or spinach is also good. Raw bits of ground beef are especially prized.

These have to be given in moderation, and need to be diced or shredded so that they will be edible for your fish. Don't just throw a shrimp in—it will either sink to the bottom or float, or one of your fish will probably end up choking on it.

Don't offer your fish your table scraps unless they conform to what is listed. Also, no spices. For sure, if you want sick fish, feed them Mexican, French or Italian cuisine. Table food needs to be plain and chopped up. Also, any condiments that you put on your food will be floating around the aquarium and could possibly poison or injure your fish.

> **TYPES OF FISH**
>
> There are three types of fish: carnivores, herbivores and omnivores. Carnivores only eat other fish or live food. Piranhas, for example, only eat other fish or other animals. Many fish enthusiasts actually feed common goldfish to piranhas. They will also eat hamburger, bits of luncheon meat and an assortment of other solid or table foods, which they tear apart with their teeth. Herbivores eat only vegetable matter. They will eat flake foods and many types of vegetable matter, including the plants in your tank. An excellent example of these is Angelfish. Goldfish are omnivores. They will eat flakes, live food and bits of table food. Basically, they will eat almost anything; however, they rarely eat anything as large as another fish in the same way an adult piranha or Oscar will.

How to Feed Your Fish

The biggest problem when feeding goldfish is that they will eat to the point of bursting. They are gluttons—and that's the nicest thing that can be said about their table manners. Their food intake must be controlled. It is best to feed goldfish about as much as they can eat in a five-minute time period. It's best to do this twice a day, morning and night, and always in the same spot.

To begin, put some flake food on the water and let them eat. If they finish all or most of it before the five minutes is up, add a little more and a little more as best you can judge until you feel that they have had enough. It's the same thing with live, freeze-dried or table food. It's that easy.

If you go away for a weekend, don't worry about feeding the fish. They can last up to three weeks without being fed. You should not abuse them because of this; however, weekend trips shouldn't cause you too much worry.

RULES FOR FEEDING GOLDFISH

1. Only feed them what they can eat in five minutes' time.
2. Feed them at the same time every day, once in the morning, once at night.
3. Always feed them at the same spot in the tank.
4. Don't overfeed the fish, no matter how humane you think you are being. More goldfish die, especially older ones, from overeating than from anything else.

SAMPLE DIET

Following is a sample diet for a 30-day period. This is not hard and fast, but is merely suggested as a way for you to gauge how you might want to vary their diet. Things can be substituted, of course, but you must make sure to balance one group with another.

You need not attempt to feed every different kind of food to your goldfish. If you buy any kind of worms or cultivate anything on your own, that month or two will have a steady diet of that particular kind of food. In the diet below, I have supposed that I have cultivated my own brine shrimp and earthworms. Along with dried food as the staple, I will attempt to mix in a few vegetables and a few more easily gotten proteins. Of course, any foods might be substituted, and I am only showing this to try to provide beginners with a possible scenario.

Day 1	Dried food	Day 16	Earthworms
Day 2	Earthworms	Day 17	Dried food
Day 3	Dried food	Day 18	Brine shrimp
Day 4	Brine shrimp	Day 19	Dried food
Day 5	Dried food	Day 20	Raw, torn spinach
Day 6	Raw, torn spinach	Day 21	Dried food
Day 7	Dried food	Day 22	Canned clams
Day 8	Cooked egg yolks	Day 23	Earthworms
Day 9	Earthworms	Day 24	Dried food
Day 10	Dried food	Day 25	Baked beans
Day 11	Brine shrimp	Day 26	Dried food
Day 12	Dried food	Day 27	Canned clams
Day 13	Baked beans	Day 28	Dried food
Day 14	Dried food	Day 29	Raw ground-beef
Day 15	Dried food	Day 30	Earthworms

chapter 7

Maintaining

Your

Aquarium

The two most important things to do with an already-operating fish tank are two of the most enjoyable. First, turn the aquarium light on and off every day. Light is important both for the fish and the plants. And as we have already learned, fish need their sleep. Second, remember to feed your fish every day. You need to do

this at the same spot of the tank each time and around the same time each morning and night.

The most important thing that any fish hobbyist can do, other than these two things, is be observant. You must closely watch the fish for signs of disease and watch their interaction to see if any are being picked on by the rest. You must check the plants to see if any parts of them are dying; if they are, these brown sections must be removed at once. You must check the water temperature to make sure that it remains constant.

You need to examine the airstone, the filter and the heater to make sure they are all in working order. The filter may be experiencing some blockage, especially if you are using a box filter. The thermostat light should be on. Make sure the airstone is operating at maximum efficiency.

General Maintenance

Cleaning a fish tank involves elbow grease. In fact, maintaining a fish tank is not for the lazy at heart. Concern must be shown at every step and every level. Your fishes' lives depend on your attention to detail.

It is important to clean away the surface film of algae and dirt. Here a magnetized scraper is used.

Vacuuming

Vacuuming is one of the most important parts of maintaining your tank. You must prevent the buildup of mulm in the gravel. Mulm is a combination of fish wastes, plant fragments and uneaten food that decay at the bottom of your tank. It is very important to clean this up because it creates nitrites and nitrates, neither of which your fish need. It also clogs up the filters and builds up on the gravel.

Vacuuming is important even if you have an underground filter because you don't want the mulm getting caught in the gravel and preventing a flow of water through the filter.

CHECK THE FILTER

Remember to check the filter medium. The top-level matt gets dirty quickly and easily, as this is the stage that collects the largest pieces of debris. If there is a buildup in your box or power filter here, it will reduce the flow of water through the filter and reduce the filter's effectiveness.

Rinse the matt off at least quarterly. Maybe you'll want to replace it at the half-year mark and then again at the year mark. Replacing it is not always necessary. There are certain bacteria that build up in your filter that are beneficial to the filtering process. A good rinse is satisfactory.

SCRAPE ALGAE

Another important thing to do is algae scraping. Algae is the soft brown/green moss that develops all over your tank. It develops faster in some tanks than in others, depending on your tank's proximity to real sunlight. Algae scrapers are either sponges attached to long stick or are a pair of magnetized scrapers that will help you to clean the inside of the aquarium walls so that you can see better inside. It is important to stop too much algae growth. At lower levels, algae perform the same beneficial tasks that all plants do. However, algae can overrun your tank.

Never use soap to clean anything in your tank. Water and elbow grease are always the best weapons against dirt and algae.

TEST THE WATER

In the beginning, water testing is very important. For the first two months, check the water every two weeks.

After that, there will be sufficient bacteria buildup for you to have what is known as a mature tank. After this takes place, you can reduce your testing to once a month.

Water Changes

A water change is when you literally take out a quarter, a third, or half of the existing water and replace it with distilled water. The amount you change is up to you, depending on the water quality of your tank. Water changes are one of the most important aspects of cleaning and maintaining your tank. Goldfish are messy fish in many instances and so water maintenance is important.

Water changes go a long way toward maintaining good water quality. Water changes are also beneficial

Siphoning:

Step 2

because you can dilute the amount of nitrites and nitrates in the water, as well as other harmful gases and substances, and the water you add is probably more oxygen rich than water that has been in your tank for some time.

Change the water after you have cleaned everything else. To do this, you must first siphon water off so that you can later add new water. To siphon water you need a long (three feet), thick tube or a hand-pump siphon, and a large bucket.

How to Siphon

1. Fill the tube up with water until it's ready to over-flow at both ends, making sure there is no trapped air anywhere in the tube. Place your thumbs over the ends of the tube on either side.

2. With your thumbs still holding the water in, place one end of the tube in the tank and aim the other end of the tube at the bucket. Make sure the bucket is lower than the tank or siphoning will not work.

3. Release your thumbs and the water will begin to flow.

Some hobbyists use the siphon to vacuum the bottom of the tank. This kills two birds with one stone. Either way, you must do both. Make sure that the water you add to your tank is not straight from the faucet, but rather, has been aged at least twenty-four to forty-eight hours. Either keep a bunch of one-gallon jugs stored somewhere in the house, or make sure to keep a five-gallon bucket somewhere that has been filled with water for several days.

A water changer can be used to siphon and to refill the tank while maintaining acceptable water conditions.

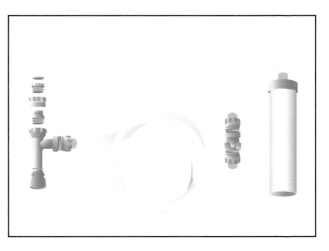

Water Changers

There are devices that can be hooked up to your tank that will change the water for you on a constant basis. Whether you have chlorinated water or not, your local pet shop will be able to fit you with one of these, should you want one. It makes life much easier but requires that you have a faucet constantly available somewhere relatively near your aquarium. Water changers are great labor-saving devices and make maintenance that much easier and life better for your fish.

Maintenance Checklists

DAILY

- Feed the goldfish twice a day.
- Turn the tank lights on and off.
- Check the water temperature.
- Check the heater and make sure the thermostat light is on.
- Make sure the filters are still in working order.
- Make sure the aerator is working.

WEEKLY

- Study the fish for diseases by observing them closely in the tank.
- Change approximately 10 percent of the aquarium water.
- Add distilled water to make up for any evaporated water.
- Check the filter to see if the top matt needs to be replaced.
- Vacuum the tank thoroughly, and attempt to clean up all mulm.
- Test the water for pH, nitrates and softness (first two months).
- Trim any brown portions of live plants.

MONTHLY

- Change 25 percent of the water; replace with distilled water.

- Clean the tank's glass on inside using an algae scraper.
- Vacuum the tank thoroughly, stirring up the gravel and eliminating mulm.
- Trim any brown portions of plants and replace them if necessary.
- Test the water for pH, nitrates and softness.
- Wash off any tank decorations that suffer from dirt buildup.

QUARTERLY

- Change 50 percent of the water; replace with distilled water.
- Replace the airstones.
- Rinse the filter materials completely and change them if necessary.
- Wash the gravel in really dirty places.
- Clean the glass on the inside using an algae scraper.
- Vacuum the tank thoroughly, stirring up the gravel and eliminating mulm.
- Trim any brown portions of plants and replace them if necessary.
- Test the water for pH, nitrates and softness.
- Wash off any decorations that suffer from dirt buildup

YEARLY

- Do a total strip-down; replace the filter medium with new matt and charcoal.
- Replace the airstones.
- Wash the gravel entirely.
- Clean the inside of the tank thoroughly.
- Start up all over again.

ONE-YEAR CLEANING CYCLE

January	Monthly
February	Monthly
March	**Quarterly**
April	Monthly
May	Monthly
June	**Quarterly**
July	Monthly
August	Monthly
September	**Quarterly**
October	Monthly
November	Monthly
December	**Yearly**

Your
Goldfish's

part three

Health

chapter 8

Breeding
Your
Goldfish

Please read this entire chapter thoroughly before making your decision to breed. Breeding is expensive, time-consuming and ultimately the most rewarding experience any goldfish hobbyist can ever have; however, breeding takes much time and preparation.

Why Breed?

There is one thing that should be said up front about breeding—don't do it thinking that you can make any money. Breeding goldfish is a money-losing prospect for the home hobbyist. Goldfish are bred in farms on every continent all over the world. They are sold very cheaply and the market will only pay what it has to. Sometimes there is a run in the spring and summer, and you can buy Common Goldfish by the dozen cheaper than you can buy two or three. So, don't do it thinking you're going to make money. To do a professional job, you need to lay out lots of cash.

Then, why breed? Well, why not? For anyone who has mastered the ability to operate a quality aquarium successfully, it is the next challenge. In fact, there are only three reasons anyone wants to breed goldfish. The first reason is because it is the next step in the mastery of aquaria. The second reason is to produce high-quality, or show-quality, goldfish of a particular variety. And the third, which is mainly a challenge for professional breeders, is to create a new and never-before-seen variety.

If You're Interested

For anyone who is interested in breeding, especially for the first time, I suggest that you stick to the first reason. Just see if you can do it. Breeding at home is fun, and not too expensive. While it may come easily in nature, it does not come so naturally in captivity.

For your first subjects, choose Common or Comet Goldfish. The reason for this is twofold. First, the Common or Comets are some of the easiest goldfish to breed, and should give you the fewest problems. Second, to breed high-quality goldfish, you must start out with high-quality goldfish. To start out with a not-so-perfect pair of Ryunkins and think you are going to breed champions out of them is wrong. The choice of high-quality breeding fish in the marketplace is not good. Professional breeders usually keep these for themselves, to renew and replenish their own stock, in order to continue breeding themselves. Buying high-quality exotics is an extremely expensive endeavor.

What to Expect

There are two spawning results that also make one rethink breeding for high quality. First, goldfish suffer many mutations in one spawn or hatch. Fry are the postlarval brood of the spawning goldfish. In a hatch of thirty-five to fifty goldfish you will find many that have malformed fins or are missing fins. Others will have deformed bodies, deformed heads, or numerous other defects. So, in a batch of thirty-five to fifty, as many as one-third of the fry could be deformed or ill. Second, according to the Goldfish Society of America's *Official Guide to Goldfish:* "They [goldfish] have a habit of reverting back to their ancestral form, i.e., olive green colored, long bodied, single finned crucian carp."

For your first breeding, choose a Common (pictured here) or a Comet because these varieties should give you the least problems.

This brings us back to the idea that if you want to breed high-quality goldfish, you need an exceptional pair to begin with, as goldfish parents tend to pass down their characteristics directly. If you breed a malformed goldfish, more than likely there will be a good number of fry that exhibit this same malformation.

For the home hobbyist there is only one real reason to breed— because it will bring pleasure to you and your family. Breeding is an exciting experience for anyone who loves being a fish— especially a goldfish— hobbyist.

So, let's begin with our pair of Common or Comet Goldfish. We have a lot to do. Not only do you need to know how goldfish spawn before you attempt this, but you also need to set up alternative tanks and learn new feeding methods.

Outcrossing

The one hard-and-fast rule in breeding goldfish is: There are no hard-and-fast rules. Given all the oddities in goldfish, there are only guidelines. However, if you are attempting to outcross (breed together two unrelated fish), there are genetic rules you should know. In outcrossing, you are generally attempting to join the best characteristics of the two unrelated parents. What you will eventually do is breed the first generation back to one or both of the parent fish, so as to increase the complimentary characteristics of the new fish.

Don't outcross without being serious about your goals. Outcrossing requires a very solid plan and a very solid end goal. Outcrossing is time-consuming and will require patience of the utmost kind. Creating a breed of any kind, whether it is one never before seen or one too difficult to find commercially, will require years of work.

The following is a sample plan that will pass on the strong characteristics in two parent fish and then attempt to reinforce those characteristics. I have labeled the generations so that you can better understand what is being explained. Notice the time element involved.

Year 1:
| Parent1 | + | Parent2 | = | First generation |

Year 3:
| Parent1 | + | First Generation | = | Second Generation (1) |
| Parent2 | + | First Generation | = | Second Generation (2) |

Year 5:
| First Gen. | + | Second Gen. (1) | = | Third Generation (1) |
| First Gen. | + | Second Gen. (2) | = | Third Generation (2) |

In all likelihood, only a few fry of the first generation will be worth breeding back to the original pair. This will go for each successive generation. In the end, what you are trying to accomplish is to mate those fish that exhibit exceptional characteristics to give you the desired end result.

This all takes time. The first generation will not be able to spawn for two years or more, depending on what you are attempting to create. By the time you get to the third generation, five years have passed, and in all likelihood you will have many goldfish. Outcrossing can be very discouraging and is recommended for only very serious hobbyists.

Spawning Is a Year-round Process

Planning spawning takes time and cannot be accomplished within a few weeks of your decision. Spawning is a year-round process, and is sometimes called conditioning. Actually, what you need to do is to vary the temperature of the aquarium for several months at a time to simulate nature's timetable.

WINTERIZING YOUR FISH

Since in nature spawning generally takes place in mid-spring to early summer, you need to "winter" your goldfish before you can contemplate spawning them. For example, in the late summer and autumn months you should feed them foods higher in carbohydrates. Flake foods, corn, breadcrumbs, bits of precooked pastina macaroni and the like are excellent choices. This simulates the storage of fat needed in nature to survive the winter months.

In the winter, with the water temperature lowered, goldfish will need less food. Feed them enough for what would be eaten in four or four and a half minutes twice a day instead of the usual five minutes. Make sure to vary their diets.

CHANGING TANK TEMPERATURES

As discussed in previous chapters, during some number of months, usually during the winter months, the temperature in the tank should be cooler. Your tank should be in the high 50°F for at least two or three months. In the spring, say March or April, the water temperature should rise slightly, to around 68°F to 74°F, then spawning is induced.

At this time you should be feeding your goldfish slightly more in the amount of food and in the type of foods. But don't just dump more food in. Instead of feeding them enough for what they would eat in five minutes, make it enough for six minutes, during each feeding.

But make sure not to overfeed them. Protein-filled foods are best. Egg, beef, seafood, beans, brine shrimp and earthworms are all excellent foods at this time.

GIVING THEM ROOM

The more space the fish have during the year, the better conditioned they are, the more active they are and the more likely you will be to get better and more fry.

Setting Up the Tank

There are two ways you can do this: aquarium breeding (also known as separate-tank breeding) and hand-stripping. Some people also pond breed, but that is another subject (see chapter 10). Aquarium breeding is the type most commonly practiced. We'll tackle aquarium breeding first.

AQUARIUM BREEDING

For the first-timer, I suggest that you use your spawning tank as your hatchery. Some experts don't like to do this, suggesting that whatever diseases or other contaminants were left behind by the parents will affect the fry. If you are breeding any type of hardy goldfish—for example, Common, Comets, Fantails or even Black Moors—this should not present a problem. Even among the other goldfish you will most likely not have a problem.

Depending on the characteristics you wish to foster, breeding can be a long and tedious process. Shown here is a Super Hamanashiki.

If you are breeding champion goldfish, especially anything rare, I would suggest taking all possible precautions by setting up a separate hatchery that has been thoroughly cleaned out and stocked with distilled water and new filters with new media, etc. No matter, if you have any kind of decent turn-out, you will probably need at least two hatchery tanks, especially if you are to go through a culling or two.

Remember, the tank needs to be very roomy. The rule of one inch of fish per one gallon of water is not enough. Two six-inch goldfish will need a thirty-gallon tank for proper mating. However, this will evolve into an excellent hatchery.

THE SPAWNING TANK

The spawning tank is where you will be mating the goldfish and hatching and raising the fry. It should be long and low, allowing for as much swimming length as possible. The tank needs only a box or power filter and an aerator. It probably does not need a heater if you are following the seasons; some experts prefer it. Again, if you have champions or other exotics, then I expect you to take all precautions. However, for a simple breeding tank, all you need is the above. Gravel, rocks and other decorations will prove quite cumbersome, so don't include these. After the mating takes place, you will need to remove the parents immediately. Later on, when culling the fry, you will need to extract some more fish. A decorated hatchery will be too difficult to navigate with a fishnet.

The water for this tank should have been distilled for at least two days and should have been with an operating filter for at least a week. Many experts suggest putting some salt in the water at this time, but you may make your own decision. Some experts prefer to place one teaspoon of salt for every five gallons of water. This is done in a hospital tank in many cases to deal with different diseases. This is much like disinfecting the water before breeding. However, I think this is somewhat overdoing it. I prefer to err on the side of caution. You might send your own fish into shock unless you treat your tank with this kind of stimulus regularly, which I do not recommend. If you must, I suggest that you add one level teaspoon of salt for each ten gallons of water. And make sure you wait a few days before adding the fish themselves.

THE FILTERS

If you are going to use the spawning tank as a hatchery,
then you will need to take certain precautions. What
you don't want happening is your fry getting sucked up
into the filter. Box filters, and especially power filters,
are notorious for this. A friend of mine once thought
he had lost one of his baby neons in a tropical tank. He
was angry, thinking his aggressive angelfish had con-
sumed the poor thing. A week later we found the neon
living quite happily in the outbox of the power filter. It
had been sucked up by the power filter's intake
siphon. Fry are even smaller and are more likely to get
pulled into a filter. They are not yet fully developed
and often don't have enough strength to get away.

If you are using a power filter, then you will need to
fit the intake valve with a sponge specially made for
such things. These are easily bought at pet stores
and through catalogs. If you are using a box filter,
then you need to use a well-conditioned sponge or a
quilt-batting cover. Some experts prefer to use both.
The idea is to save as many fry from themselves
as possible.

In the first few days after the eggs hatch, I suggest that
you shut the filters off for a minute twice a day for the
first three to five days in order to free any fry not
strong enough to extract themselves from the filter. A
large number of weak or malformed fry will in all likelihood die off—Darwin's law of nature is everywhere.
As a breeder, you want to ensure that you don't kill too
many of the healthy ones all by yourself.

PLANTS AND SPONGES

You will need plants in the spawning tank, and you
will need live plants for spawning. Foxtail and hornwort are the two best. Some breeders leave these to
float in bunches at the top as well as having some that
have been anchored.

Some hobbyists prefer breeding sponges, also known
as spawning mops. These are floating sponges that are

shredded but bunched at the end, and that float on the surface or near the surface of the water. They will never die, as live plants might. And again, some people are extremely afraid to use live plants, especially ones not home-grown, as no one knows what diseases or fungi they might be carrying. Both sponges and plants in spawning tanks are known as spawning media.

Don't place them all over the tank. Floating plants are generally anchored to the top of the aquarium so that they don't float around. The plants on the floor of the aquarium should also be anchored. Place the floating and anchored plants in one corner of the tank so that the eggs will not be all over the place. Generally, place them in the corner opposite the filter.

There are many qualities to consider when selecting a pair of goldfish for breeding.

WHICH FISH?

As the old adage goes: Age before beauty. You really want goldfish that are between two and four or five years old. Any fish younger cannot or should not be bred because it is not yet mature. Likewise, any fish beyond four or five years old are past their prime and may not pass on their best qualities.

Differentiating Males and Females   The only time you'll really be able to differentiate males from females is during mating season. Before that it is very difficult.

Breeding season is spring and early summer. At this time most females will take on a rounder shape, and will appear especially thick when viewed from above. This is because they are carrying eggs. Males, on the other hand, will appear slimmer. Male goldfish will grow something like pimples on their gills, called *tubercles*. On some fish these will even exhibit themselves on the head or pectoral fins. Days before spawning, the males will exhibit very aggressive behavior, chasing the females all around the tank. After mating season passes, the tubercles will disappear.

CHOOSING THE PAIR

Make sure you choose fish that exhibit the best qualities of the breed. Consider finnage, shape, size, and color in both the male and the female. Make sure the finnage is complete and correct. Make sure the body is the right shape. And make sure the fish are of the correct size. There is no use in breeding small goldfish. Make sure that your mating specimens are healthy and do not suffer from stunted growth. Two-year-old male and female Common or Comet Goldfish, if raised in a large enough tank, should be from four to six inches in length. Make sure that there are no deformities of any kind, and make sure that their coloration is good.

> ### EGG EATERS
>
> Goldfish are notorious egg eaters. As soon as it is apparent that the spawning is over, remove the male and female from the tank to keep them from eating the eggs. Additionally, if you are using two males and one female and one of the males seems disinterested, after a while remove him. He will only end up eating the eggs.

Coloration is always important in breeding goldfish. And this brings up an often-controversial subject: It is not important to breed fish that show exceptional color the fastest. Many commercial breeders tend to breed those fish that reach their deepest colors at a younger age. They do this only for reasons of commerce. It's always easiest to sell the most colorful fish.

But if you are breeding, especially if you are looking to show, it is not necessary to chose those fish that reach their deepest colors at an early age. Many champion goldfish are, in fact, late bloomers, whose real colors do not show up until the fish are two or three years of age. Commercial breeders are just trying to sell their stock as quickly as possible. As a home breeder, this should not be a consideration for you. Breed for deepest color, not fastest.

TANK DIVIDERS OR SEPARATE TANKS

Many people separate the males from the females just before spawning. This is accomplished in one of two ways: by using either a tank divider or two separate tanks. Placing the males and females in separate areas before spawning gives the breeder a chance to really control the situation.

Dividers can be purchased at your pet store or through catalogs. By placing the two fish or three fish in the breeding tank while the divider is still up, you can guard against the fishes' mating when you are not around. You will be able to monitor their spawning, and exercise greater control.

There is no real advantage to separate tanks for the home hobbyist unless you are attempting to breed many goldfish. In this case, you may want one tank for females and one tank for males, using the spawning tank only for spawning, and removing both the adult fish and the eggs after spawning.

Mating Naturally

Goldfish do not pair off. Being egglayers, they are not particularly choosy about who they mate with as much as about how they are courted. As the critical time arrives, the males will begin chasing the females around the tank. This is known as *driving*. The males will eventually drive the females into some plant life.

This is why it is important to have plants in the tank during spawning. It is here, as the male starts to rub against the female with his tubercles, among some foxtail, hornwort or other plants, that the spawning actually takes place. At this time the male and female respectively discharge their sperm and eggs into the water. As the eggs attach themselves to the plants, the sperm floating free in the water around them fertilizes them.

There are two methods that can be followed here:

One Male, One Female   If you are attempting to breed prize-winning goldfish or you have an exceptional pair of parents, using only one male and one female ensures the hobbyist that the characteristics of the two parents will be directly passed on to the fry. This method guarantees the most control any hobbyist can have over Mother Nature's territory.

If you are attempting to cross-breed two different varieties, also known as line breeding, it is almost imperative that you follow this method, so as to ensure some amount of quality control.

Two Males, One Female   As I said before, these fish are egglayers and they do not mate for life. Some breeders, especially commercial breeders, will put their best two males in the same tank with their best female to ensure that as many eggs as possible get fertilized. Quality control is at a minimum here, as the hobbyist cannot dictate the number of eggs that will be fertilized by each male. The chances are, however, that you will end up with a lot more fry. Commercial breeders use this method to produce quantity. If you are just trying to breed for the first time, and you are following my suggestion of using Common or Comet Goldfish, then this method will ensure that you have as many fertilized eggs as possible.

CHOOSING WHEN TO MATE

When you have decided the time has come to mate, drop two ice cubes into the tank for every ten gallons of water. Wait for the ice cubes to melt and then remove the divider. The change in the water temperature is thought to stimulate goldfish spawning. If you do this, make sure you have a heater in the tank that is set for anywhere from 66°F to 74°F. If you do this at night, the water will warm by morning, and there should be eggs. If there are not, leave the fish. Sometimes it takes a couple of days. Monitor the situation as carefully as you can.

Goldfish usually mate in the morning. If nothing has happened by midday, then nothing will probably happen until the next morning. You may need to repeat this course of action over a week's time or more to get the desired response. Sometimes it happens right away, sometimes not. *C'est l'amour!*

After they have mated, put the parents back into the divided tank for a day or two and then reintroduce them back into their original tank.

Hand-stripping

Hand-stripping. In the same bowl, strip the male first (A). After moving the water around to distribute the sperm, strip the female (B) right away.

This is a technique really only used by professionals at fish farms, wildlife fisheries, and commercial aquaria. Some experts also argue that it is sometimes necessary when breeding some of the fancier or more exotic fish. Hand-stripping ensures that there will be no loss in the number of eggs produced because they have been eaten.

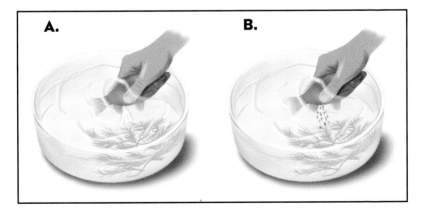

This process is somewhat more dangerous to the fish and thus this method should really be used only by experts. All the preceding steps must be followed, even when hand-stripping. There are no saved steps. If you begin hand-stripping and the eggs or sperm (milt) do not come easily, don't force anything. This is a very easy way for you to kill your own goldfish, or at least injure them severely.

Some people carry out this process in a pail or in a small, open bowl and then transfer the spawning medium with the fertilized eggs into the hatchery. Hand-stripping should be done this way for the best results. In the bowl, place enough water to partially submerge your goldfish and a bunch of foxtail or a spawning mop.

Take the male first, and hold him gently in your hand in the water. Carefully squeeze the area on the body between the ventral and anal fins. Sperm should come out very easily. When this is accomplished, move the water around so that the sperm is evenly distributed, especially in the area with the plants. Immediately remove the male and repeat the same exact process with the female. Again, you must be very careful and gentle with these fish in order not to injure or kill them. The eggs should come out very easily.

After this is accomplished, pour the eggs and plants and water into the hatchery. Some experts advocate submerging the entire bowl into the hatchery, as goldfish eggs will cling to the walls of the bowl. I highly recommend it.

Multiple Spawning

If you want more eggs than you got, or if you are interested in performing additional breeding of your fish, the male and female will be more than happy to spawn for you again. Place them back in the divided tank and continue to feed them high-protein foods. Then place them back together every seven to ten days. They should start mating again without incident during the spawning season.

If you continue mating the same pair in the same tank, make sure that you change some of the water at one point or another. In high concentrations, goldfish sperm is not good for goldfish. If you are attempting multiple spawnings, make sure you change the water in the parents' tank at least once a week.

Eggs

The water temperature in a hatchery is very important. While the eggs will eventually hatch, the water should be kept between 66°F and 74°F. This means that the eggs should hatch in anywhere from three and a half to five days. The colder the water, the longer it takes for the fry to hatch.

Healthy eggs are round and clear—these are fertile. Some eggs will not be clear, but will appear white or tan and will be opaque—these have not been fertilized. An egg fungus, somewhat white and furry, will develop on the eggs that are not fertile or infected. These will be easily detectable in twenty-four hours.

Remove unfertilized eggs from the tank as soon as possible to avoid any complications. As I mentioned before, adding salt to the tank should cut down on the chances that this will happen. But removing nonproducing eggs as quickly as possible is the only safe bet. Fertile eggs remain so clear that you can watch them develop. Within two days you should be able to detect what will be eyes inside each tiny egg.

Caring for the Fry

The First Two Days When the eggs actually hatch, the young fry will appear motionless for two days. Don't move them. Basically they look like two small eyes attached to a piece of glass. They are very slight and do not need to be fed. They live off the yolk sac.

This is the easiest time as the hobbyist needs to do nothing for the first two days. It is important not to disturb your fry until they start moving of their own accord. Do not stir them up. They will begin moving under their own power, so do not attempt to agitate them on your own. Do as little as possible to ensure that you don't ruin this important hatching phase.

Days Three to Ten It is important that scum does not develop on the surface of the water in the hatchery. You should have an aerator in the tank, and that should do a great deal to prevent the scum from settling on the surface. No matter, you should skim the top of the tank a couple of times. Why?

The first movement goldfish make is toward the surface. They take a gulp of air. Many experts feel that this is an attempt to fill the swim bladder. Adult goldfish will sometimes do the same. If the surface is filled with scum, the bladders in these young fry will become injured—the fish will have problems swimming properly and will become what some goldfish hobbyists term *belly sliders.*

After two or three days the fry will begin to move around looking for food. They will begin doing this not by swimming toward the surface, but by swimming horizontally across the tank, back and forth. They really dart.

At this stage, some experts encourage you to turn up the heat by about 2°F to 4°F. It is thought that this encourages appetite and activity among the fry, which will induce them to eat.

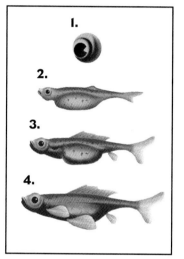

Feeding Fry

At this point you must begin to feed your fry. This should be done three times a day: once in the morning, once at midday and once at night, but not just before bedtime. Give the fish a chance to eat. You can enjoy observing them and then you can clean up any debris before you leave the tank for the night. Also, the fry are not experienced eaters and they need light to see their food.

Stages of embryo development.

(1) 24 hours

(2) 5 days

(3) 7 days

(4) 10 days

If you really want excellent goldfish, you should not feed them flake food. Live food will garner the best results. My recommendations are baby brine shrimp, ground earthworms, crushed bean paste, crushed yolk of hard-boiled egg, or other commercially produced liquid foods which should be available through catalogs or at your pet shop. All the above-mentioned solid foods must be ground down into a dry flourlike texture or into a paste. With egg, feed only a little at a time, as

117

egg yolk will likely cause a fouling of the water if overused.

You can, however, also use dry flake food—this is an acceptable food. As the fry get older, you will probably mix in more and more of this staple. You need to grind it up to a powdery consistency. Make sure that you buy the best possible food to ensure that your fish are getting the best possible diet.

Many experts agree that you should feed your fry live food, as it is high in protein. They don't, however, always agree on what live food to feed them. Some recommend tubifex or bloodworms, while others recommend microworms or daphnia. Many also shy away from these foods as the fry are so young that they may not be strong enough to fight off any diseases or fungus associated with those foods. Why risk it when you have planned so long for such an event?

LINE BREEDING

Different varieties of goldfish are actually mutations. Breeders create the varieties by breeding goldfish exhibiting certain desired malformations which are then passed along to the fry. If this continues, you have a new variety! It is for this very same reason that some exotic rare breeds sometimes nearly disappear, and then are brought back, as mutations are bred together again to form a new strand, which is really an old strand that disappeared because of lack of good breeding specimens. Because all goldfish are classified Carassius auratus, they are all the same species—all the various varieties interbreed. Cross-breeding for a desired mutation is called line breeding.

FEEDING INFUSORIA

One of the best foods you can feed the newest fry is infusoria. Infusoria is a bacterial culture that your fry will love. Easily digestible and very nutritious, it is truly one of the best foods available for such small fish.

You should begin making infusoria when the eggs are three days old. Remember when feeding not to overfeed, as you do not need to cloud the tank with uneaten foods. Remember to skim any uneaten food off the water surface after five minutes and vacuum the tank once a day, or at least once every other day. Food debris can collect at the bottom of the tank and create bacteria and ammonia you do not need in your hatchery. When you vacuum or skim, make sure that you don't accidentally snag any of the fry.

To make infusoria, fill a jar approximately three quarters full with cooled-down boiled water. At this time add a banana peel or three or four lettuce leaves (it's best when the lettuce leaves are bruised, usually the outside leaves on a head of day-old lettuce). With the lid off, place the jar in a relatively sunny spot, but don't keep it in the kitchen, because this stuff will stink.

For the first few days the water will be cloudy and will smell simply awful. But in a day or two more the water will clear up and, while it still won't smell pretty, it will have a sweetness you can easily detect. Voilà! Infusoria. You can use a turkey baster or a spoon to feed the infusoria into the tank, or you can just pour some in.

If you want to use infusoria, you need to make a new jar of it every two to three days, so that you will be able to feed your fry without running out.

Culling

As previously discussed, breeding will result in only a handful of excellent specimens. Some whole batches of fry don't even add up to that. Regardless, the average batch of fry is more than twenty-five goldfish, which means that if you only end up keeping the five or six best, you need to do something with the rest.

Culling is the act of making a cut in the number of goldfish you have—separating the good specimens from the bad, or from the different. During the course of the next thirty to sixty days you should constantly be looking for those fish that best exemplify the best characteristics of the variety you have chosen to breed. You will keep those and cull the rest.

At 10 Days   The first culling takes place ten days after spawning. At this stage you need to remove any fish that are misshapen, deformed or missing eyes or fins, have misshapen fins, or are otherwise unacceptable. Any fish that are unusually small must also be culled. Culling at this stage is somewhat difficult. At best the most you can remove are those fish whose deformities are very obvious. It is too early to make many other judgments.

Culling is a difficult thing. If you have to think about whether a fish is going to make the cut, don't sweat it—it should be culled. If you are attempting to raise excellent fancies, you need to be as critical as possible. Home-grown varieties tend to be the best specimens, so it's important to keep that in mind when culling.

What to do with the culled fish? This is the worst part of fish raising. Some experts use the fry at this early stage as live food for their largest goldfish. Others give them to local pet shops, which use them for the same purpose. Still others pour them into local fish ponds, where they will probably meet the same fate. Regardless, these fish are malformed or are runts and would probably not survive in nature.

As the fish get older and you are separating better goldfish from mediocre goldfish, you can give the culled fish to your local pet shop. Many shops will take them gladly, and some might even offer you a slight store credit for well-raised commercial stock if you keep them long enough (I'll get to that later).

At One to Two Months This is the second important culling time. As the fish grow, more and more they resemble the fish they are supposed to be. Culling at this stage can even become a daily event.

The most important culling takes place after about thirty days, when you begin to see that some fish are significantly larger than the others. If they are not separated, the smaller fish will be eaten by the larger ones. A culling is usually done here to extract the larger ones from the smaller ones. As the fry begin to be culled, you need to examine how many you actually want to keep. To keep one third of the fry you will need at least three tanks, so it is important to know how many you actually want to keep. The rest may go to any of the above places.

At this time, the foods you feed your fry will begin to change as well. Flake food will be mixed in more often, and the size of the foods you feed will shade more toward the adult as well.

It is now that more highly discerning breeders begin their truest cullings. Whatever the breed, always have a good picture in your mind of what the epitome of the breed looks like when you are culling. Have that end goal in mind. Here are a few helpful hints.

CULLING BY COLORATION

Metallic Varieties At sixty days metallic fry will begin to lose their olive-green color and become a pale orange or yellow. They sometimes get darker just before they change color. To improve color, sunlight is very important to goldfish, as are water temperature and diet, as we have already discussed in previous chapters. Any fish that does not have a relatively deep color by twelve months of age should be culled.

Nacreous or Calico Varieties These will start to develop colors in their second month. While blues usually show up much later, orange and black are usually the first colors. Some experts recommend that you keep your top calicos at least two years before making the final culling, as their colors change over time. Darker colors in young fish tend to stick, and as stated previously, these are thought to be the most highly prized of these types.

Matt Varieties Matt varieties of any breed are usually wonderfully different. They can easily be picked out by their solid black eyes and flat pink bodies. These can be picked out at quite a young age.

CULLING BY VARIETY

Comets The tail should equal half the length of the body. The other fins should be long and elegant.

Fantails   Fantails should not have humped backs, but should be straight. Make sure all the fins are separate and distinct. Fantails often have fins joined along one side. These are unacceptable.

Veiltails   The Veiltails with the longest anal fins are usually the ones to keep. All finnage should be separate and distinct. The dorsal fin should be high and erect. Any joint fins are unacceptable. Some fry will look like Fantails; these must be culled.

Moors   If their color does not change from a silvery brown to a darker brownish-black by the time their eyes have developed, then they will never turn out properly.

An Oranda.

Orandas   Orandas should not have humped backs, but should be straight. Make sure all the fins are separate and distinct. Some Orandas will have fins joined along one side. These are unacceptable.

The fry will be difficult to judge, as hood growth does not begin until they are at least a year or a year and a half old. A good sign among this type is a somewhat textured appearance around the head.

Ranchus or Lionheads   The fry will be difficult to judge, as hood growth does not begin until the fish are at least a year or a year and a half old. A strong, wide back with straight lines is best. Hunched backs are acceptable. A good sign among this type is a somewhat textured appearance around the head.

Celestial   The eyes take anywhere from six months to a year to fully develop. However, good finnage and a straight back are paramount.

Bubble-eyes   As with the Celestial, the eyes take a long time to develop. However, little protruding sacs should be visible at an early age. The back should be straight and wide regardless of what finnage variety it is. If this is the Bubble-eye with a dorsal fin, the fin should be erect and relatively high.

Ryunkin   This is hunchback heaven. The bigger the hunched back, the better. The dorsal fin should be high and erect. The finnage should be distinct and not joined along any edges.

Pearl-Scales   These fish should begin showing signs of their pearl-scales quite early, making the breeder's job that much less difficult. The more area covered by the pearl-scales the better. They should have a rounded, full middle, and some hump to their back. The dorsal fin should be erect and high.

chapter 9

Diseases
of the
Goldfish

Goldfish are subject to all kinds of diseases. Many are introduced with new fish. Many diseases are highly contagious; others are not. Though you may think you did everything you possibly could to protect your fish, even experts fall victim to these problems.

Goldfish and Diseases

One of the best ways to cure any fish is to separate it from the rest of the fish as quickly as possible. It should be placed in something I call the "hospital tank." This should be set up like any other tank, with filters and aerator, but no plants or gravel should be present. The tank generally does not have to be very big. Depending on the size of your fish a ten-gallon tank is usually fine.

There are many reasons to have a hospital tank. First, many fish diseases are contagious. Anytime you think you might have a diseased fish, it's always better to separate it, at least until you can determine whether its affliction is transmittable or not. Also, diseased or weak fish will often get picked on by healthier fish. Goldfish are no exception, and their bedside manner can be less than sympathetic. And, obviously, it's easier to observe the fish when it's by itself.

Some of the below-listed problems, while they may not be contagious, will require treatment, sometimes something as simple as a change of diet. However, when you are attempting to feed your goldfish medicated food, it is important that the fish you are trying to help get it. The idea is not to overmedicate the healthy fish. This is another reason to separate out sick fish.

Another thing to know is that healthy goldfish rarely get sick. So when your fish get sick, it usually means that they have been weakened by poor water conditions, rapid temperature changes, bad lighting, bad food, or any number of other things. It is important to maintain your aquarium carefully so that, in the future, you won't have to be reading this chapter again.

A Ryunkin with mouth fungus, a cottony growth on its mouth.

Commercial Remedies

Especially for beginners, and even for some experts, I am very much in favor of using the best commercial remedies over a home mixture of chemicals. Some experts advise using malachite green or potassium permanganate. These chemicals must be handled in very exact dosages: When given in too much volume, they will easily kill your fish much faster than any disease. If possible, discuss the problem with someone at your local pet store and let that person advise you on the best commercial remedies the store carries. Follow the directions exactly. Especially with fancy goldfish, caution must be maintained.

The Old-fashioned Salt Bath

This is the most time-tested cure-all of the fish world. Sometimes called progressive salt-water treatment, it is what the hospital tank most often stands for. It is very simple and has been known to cure ich, fugus, velvet, tail rot, and other malignancies. Many experts swear by it.

Place the fish in the hospital tank and add one teaspoon of table salt (not iodized) for each gallon of water. Add the same amount of salt that night and twice the next day, again in the morning and at night. If there is no improvement by the third or fourth day, add one more teaspoon of salt each day (just one, not eleven). On the ninth and tenth days, make progressive water changes and check for results.

Emergency Cleaning

This is the most severe treatment any tank can get. If any of the infestations mentioned below strike more than three or four fish, you need to make an emergency cleaning. Place all the fish in the hospital tank and begin treatment. Then turn your attention to the aquarium.

You must begin the aquarium anew. It must be thoroughly cleaned and totally restarted. Throw out the filter medium and save as little as possible.

Empty out the contents of the tank. Rinse the walls of the tank, the gravel, and the filter with bleach. Make sure to rinse extra-thoroughly. Do the same to any plastic plants. Throw out any rocks and buy new ones. If you had any live plants, throw them out—don't use them for any other purpose. Replace the filter medium and the airstones, etc. If you have a heater, wash it with bleach as well and rinse it extra-thoroughly.

Diseases, Infestations and Pests

Constipation or Indigestion (not contagious) A fish that is constipated or suffering from indigestion is often very inactive, and usually rests at the bottom of the tank. More likely than not, its abdomen swells or bulges. This is usually a result of food that does not agree with it. You will need to change food. Some experts add one tablespoon of Epsom salt for each five gallons of water in the hospital tank. Starve the fish for three, four, or five days, until it returns to being active. When it does, feed it live or freeze-dried foods for one whole week. After one week, place it back in its normal tank. It is very likely that a fish that suffers from this problem needs to be watched, as this problem tends to recur.

If your fish is ill, such as this one with damaged gill plates, it is best to place it in a hospital tank.

This is especially a problem with Tosakins, Ryunkins, Veiltails and Pearl-Scales. Constipation and swim bladder problems must be taken seriously and treated quickly. If not, they are among the leading causes of death in goldfish.

Swim Bladder Problems (not contagious) Sometimes this results from constipation. A swim bladder problem is easy to diagnose: The fish can't swim properly. They will swim on their sides or upside-down, or will somersault as they attempt to swim. Sometimes they can be found either at the bottom or at the top of the tank. If it's a female, she might be carrying eggs. You could try hand-stripping her very gently to see if this is what has bound her up. If not, try the old-fashioned salt bath (see above).

Swim bladder problems sometimes right themselves and sometimes they don't. Like constipation or indigestion, once your fish has developed this painful problem it is more likely to experience a recurrence. Wait for the fish to right itself.

At this time you might want to feed your fish some medicated food. Your pet store owner will be able to direct you in this instance. Regardless, feed your fish something else, as diet is one of the biggest reasons this problem develops at all.

A black Lionhead with dropsy.

This happens mostly to the egg-shaped-body goldfish, both with and without dorsal fins. This problem may also occur as a result of drastic or sudden changes in temperature.

Dropsy or Kidney Bloat (also known as aeromonas; may be contagious)   This is also known as "pine cone" disease in Japan. The belly bloats noticeably and the scales stick out like a pine cone. Fish generally don't live more than a week after full-blown dropsy makes itself known. Some fish have survived. Like constipation and swim bladder problems, these fish tend to have recurring attacks. While dropsy is not thought to be contagious, it is best to remove the fish at once. The tank should receive an emergency cleaning.

Many experts still feel that dropsy is untreatable and that the fish should be immediately removed and painlessly destroyed. Others feel that medicated food is one way to treat dropsy. Still others suggest mixing

Furanace with water, 250 milligrams to the gallon. This bath should last only an hour and should not be repeated more than three times in three days. It is thought that Furanace can be absorbed by goldfish through the skin. If you decide not to use Furanance, try the old-fashioned salt bath (see above).

If there is no response after two or three days, the fish should probably be destroyed.

Tumors (usually not contagious)   Obvious lumps, bumps or protrusions, tumors sometimes look like a large blister or wart. They have been known to grow to the size of a large screw head. They can be surgically removed, but that should only be done by a veterinarian.

Pop Eye (also known as exophthalmus; not contagious)   This is difficult to diagnose, because people sometimes think they have bought the wrong fish. These fish suffer from eyes that begin to protrude in a very abnormal way. There is no cure for it. It usually happens to Common Goldfish, Comets, Shubunkins and the like. As long as the fish does not seem to suffer and goes on living a normal life, there is no reason to act.

Fish Lice (highly contagious)   There is no mistaking this ugly problem. These grotesque parasites measure about one fifth of an inch wide. They are round, disk-shaped creatures that clamp on to a host and refuse to let go. Sometimes the infected fish will rub up against objects in the tank in an effort to scrape these pests off. Some fish have been known to jump out of the water in an attempt to cleanse themselves of these ghastly crustaceans. They suck blood and other nutrients out of the fish through the skin and scales. They can sometimes be found on fins, but these are usually not quite so satisfying for them. The lice also transmit other microscopic diseases. After the parasite disengages, the part of the fish suffering the bite may become infected.

Fortunately, there are a number of quality commercial parasite-control products out on the market. Your pet store owner can help you select one. The fish should be quarantined and the tank disinfected with the same parasite control.

On larger fish, experts have been known to drip hot paraffin wax from a candle onto the parasite. Usually this is enough to get the parasite to release. Other experts recommend giving the afflicted fish a bath for fifteen minutes in a mixture of potassium permanganate and water, which should be extremely light pink. Consult your local pet store owner first. Regardless, lice are extremely treatable, but both the fish and the aquarium must be treated.

Most often recommended for aquarium treatment for fish lice, anchor worms and leeches are Dipterex, Masoten, Dylox or Nequvon. All bite marks or wounds must be treated on the fish. Dab on the spot a little Mercurochrome, malachite green or methylene blue. *Note:* Do not use Formalin in this case—its margin for error is so slim that not only will you kill the parasites, you will more than likely kill your goldfish. This should be used by professionals only.

Anchor Worm (also known as *Lernaea;* highly contagious) This is very much like the above-mentioned fish lice. The symptoms are the same. The fish will rub itself against anything it can in an attempt to scrape off the parasite. Instead of a parasite on top of the scales, the anchor worm is burrowed into the scales. It creates a red, agitated area, and from this protrudes a white worm. Sometimes these can grow quite long.

Treatment of anchor worm will include taking the fish out of water and removing the worm from the aggravated area. Follow the instructions accompanying the parasite-control product carefully.

To remove the worm: Place a wet cloth in your hand. Take hold of the fish in the hand holding the cloth. Make sure that the fish is positioned such that the worm is facing you. Then, with a pair of household tweezers, press as close into the ulcer as possible, but only extract the worm. Make sure not to rip any flesh off the fish itself. This is very dangerous to the fish and you must be extremely cautious when approaching this. It may be best to get someone experienced to do it for you.

Leeches (highly contagious) These are relatively uncommon among goldfish, but are serious once contracted. These are not the leeches that we see as free living creatures in lakes and ponds. The leeches I'm talking about are parasitic, wormlike creatures that feed on the flesh and blood of your fish. They need to be removed as quickly as possible. Don't attempt to remove them with forceps or tweezers. The leeches are quite strong and you will do more damage to your fish than the leeches by trying to pull them off. Again, call your pet store for advice on commercially produced cures.

A fish with swim bladder problems will not be able to swim properly and will often swim upside-down.

Another solution is this one: Prepare a salt bath consisting of eight level tablespoons of table salt for each gallon of water. Once the salt is sufficiently dissolved, add the fish for no more than ten minutes. The leeches that do not fall off can now be removed with tweezers or forceps quite easily.

Again, the aquarium needs to be treated immediately with commercial parasite-control chemicals. Check all your fish for just such a problem. Always isolate the infected fish.

Fluke—Skin and Gill   Like all infestations, weakened fish fall victim first. The gill fluke (*Dactylogyrus*) is very easily detectable. It causes the gills to swell up pink and red, and the fish spends lots of time near the surface trying to suck in air. Sometimes a pusslike fluid will be exuded from the gills at this time. These flukes are microscopic parasites that lodge themselves in the gills. Sometimes the fish have a severe color loss. The skin fluke (*Gyrodactylus*) gives the appearance of a swelled-up coat of some sort. As in all other parasite manifestations, the host fish is constantly trying to rub itself against objects to scrape off the infestation.

Again, pet stores have pest-control remedies for this ailment, which is more easily treatable than the ones I have already listed. Again, the tank also needs to be treated to make sure the infestation does not spread.

Some experts add formaldehyde to the water where the fish has been quarantined. Do this only if commercial solutions are unavailable or have not resulted in a cure. Place the fish in a gallon of water. Add fifteen drops of formaldehyde every minute for ten minutes. Then remove the fish and place it in the hospital tank. Repeat this process daily for three days. Don't just dump in a whole load of formaldehyde—it may kill your fish. It is important to follow the instructions and time it precisely.

Sometimes fry fall victim to this parasite. They are not strong enough to make it on their own. Make a solution of twelve tablespoons of salt to two quarts of water. Dip the fry in for thirty to forty-five seconds each. Put them in a hospital tank and repeat the process again one hour later.

Furunculosis   This bacterial infection can go for some time unnoticed, but then it will spread faster than anything you have ever seen. These bacteria infect the flesh under the scales somewhat like skin flukes. However, they first manifest themselves by raising bumps underneath the scales. A short time afterward the bumps rupture and create large bleeding ulcers. There is no certain cure for this.

While some fish have actually survived, large scars often still prove a problem for them. Fish with these kinds of ulcers probably should be destroyed. The remaining fish should be treated with Tetracycline immediately. Some experts argue that all foods should also be immediately changed and any remaining previous foods be thrown out.

If your goldfish has a tumor, it should be removed by a veterinarian.

Treatment can last up to ten days. If you have a trustworthy heater, you may want to raise the water to 80°F for that time, as furunculosis is a cold-water disease and the high temperature is thought to kill it.

Ulcers (also known as "Hole-in-the-Body" disease; highly contagious)   This is an infection that tends to be internal and that manifests itself in large red ulcers, boils and dark reddening at the bases of the fins. It cannot be mistaken for anchor worms because anchor-worm ulcers swell up, whereas these usually tend to eat away into the body.

A salt bath may be too harsh, but the affected fish should be isolated immediately. Begin feeding medicated food immediately, as well. Sometimes antibiotics are called for, but you will need a veterinarian for this. Consult your local pet store before proceeding.

Ich (also known as *Ichthyophthirius;* highly contagious) Raised white spots about the size of a salt or sugar granule appear on the body and fins. This is one of the most common parasites among fish. It should not be taken lightly, as it will kill your fish if given enough time.

There are many commercial ich remedies on the market. Many of them are good, so don't buy the cheapest one, buy the best. Remove the fish showing the symptoms and treat it in a hospital tank. However, the entire tank must be treated. Follow the directions carefully.

If an ich treatment is not available to you, raise the tank temperature to 85°F and add one teaspoon of salt for every gallon of water in the tank. Give the fish in the hospital tank the ten-day salt-water treatment. It is important to kill this organism before it has a chance to infest the entire population.

Note: If the ich spots are only on the gills of your goldfish, then you should refer to Chapter 8 on breeding, as your male goldfish may be coming into breeding season.

Velvet (also known as *Oodinium;* highly contagious) This is very difficult to detect initially, because the fuzzy area that grows has a yellow or golden color, and on a goldfish it is hard to find. Commercial treatments for this fungus are best. Some experts use malachite green or the old-fashioned salt bath. If your pet store doesn't have a commercial treatment, which it should, I suggest that you use the ten-day salt-water treatment.

Also, make sure to place some sort of antifungal chemical in the water in the aquarium, so as to disinfect the tank.

Fungus (also known as *Saprolegnia;* highly contagious) Generally a fuzzy growth, it is different from velvet because it is whiter and easier to notice. Some experts paint the affected areas with methylene blue and place the fish in a ten-day salt-water treatment.

Again, commercial treatments are usually available, either through pet stores or catalogs.

Body Slime Fungus (highly contagious)   This deadly affliction can kill your fish in two days if not caught in time. The protective slime coating I talked about earlier grows white and starts peeling off, as if the fish were shedding or molting. The fins are gradually covered as well. Eventually, the body becomes red from irritation.

Call your pet store right away—no time should be lost. Commercial cures are available, but must be found quickly. A salt bath with warm temperatures may be a temporary solution, as it may retard growth of the fungus. But a cure must be found, and a salt bath won't do it. Some people follow severe salt treatments with ich cures. This is also a good idea. *Note:* Oranda and Lionhead owners beware. In the spring or summer a whitish film will cover the heads of these fish. Be very discerning. More times than not, this is a stage of continued hood growth.

Note the raised white spots on this Black Moor, which indicate that this goldfish has ich.

Mouth Fungus (also known as *Chondrococuus;* contagious)   A white cottony growth on the mouth, this fungus sometimes spreads toward the gills. This is caused by a bacteria known as *Flexibacter.* If left untreated for any amount of time it will destroy the entire mouth region of a goldfish and lead to its eventual death.

135

Again, commercial cures are available. I strongly suggest that you follow their directions to the letter. If you want to, you can begin a salt-water treatment right away if the stores are closed or if commercial chemicals are unavailable. Some people will start a salt bath and then use a general commercial fungal or bacterial control. Consult your pet store owner once you have made your diagnosis.

Fish Pox (probably not contagious)   This affects Koi more than it does goldfish, but it's best to cover it in this chapter. Basically this is a viral infection which causes a whitish or pinkish waxy film to develop over the fish's skin and fins. The usual pattern is that it appears, gets worse and then disappears.

We have no idea what triggers it or what eventually happens. However, it does not appear to be contagious, as far as anyone can tell. Of course, you probably should separate out the infected fish until you can figure out what it is, or until the film goes away. It will usually go away within seven to ten days—with a salt treatment or without one. It's more annoying than anything else, since it does not kill the fish. However, there is no known cure either.

Fin or Tail Rot (contagious)   This is sometimes caused by fighting among your fish—the fins get damaged and then bacteria infect the injured area. Other times the fish just contract it. It is easily detectable as the fins have missing parts and gradually become shredded. Eventually, the entire fin will be eaten away, by the disease. There are many broad-spectrum medications that will help you to deal with this situation. Consult your local pet dealer.

Some experts argue that the best way to treat this is by dipping your fish for five minutes in a bath made up of eight crystals of potassium permanganate to three quarts of water. Then, you cut off the infected areas of the tail or fin and paint them with a 5 percent solution of methylene blue or Mercurochrome. Again, I feel this is only for the larger and stronger fish, and that steps like this are for experts only.

Make sure that you treat the aquarium water with some kind of medication, as this is usually contagious.

Fin Congestion (contagious)   This disease very commonly attacks goldfish, especially the long-finned breeds. It is easily identifiable because of the red blotches that appear on the trailing edges of the fins. You are looking for hemorrhages—bright-red topical areas, not veins inside the fish. Many goldfish have red blood vessels that are somewhat visible on their tails, but that's not what you are looking for. Here the blood vessels become inflamed at the ends of the tail. This disease starts at the edge of the fins and works its way toward the body, much like fin rot.

Some experts feel that fin congestion is an indication that the water quality in the tank is very poor. Change 50 percent of the water and add enough methylene blue to turn the water a very slight blue. Or add one tablespoon of rock salt for every gallon of water (sprinkle the salt around the tank over a period of a few minutes—don't just dump it all in). Either of these treatments should clear up the problem in a few days.

If these treatments don't work, then you need to purchase an antibiotic, either penicillin or Tetracycline hydrochloride. Follow the directions carefully, as these chemicals, if used too much, will become very toxic to the fish.

China Disease (also known as "Chinese rot"; highly contagious)   This is not a very common disease, and you must be absolutely sure of your diagnosis. This is the most contagious disease I have listed here. It is also the most deadly. There is no known cure for China disease.

The symptoms are very easily read. The tail fin and other fins begin to fray, very much as in fin rot. However, this time it begins at the base of the fin and works its way outward. Also, the affected areas begin to blacken. Even the ventral region begins to turn black.

In this case there is no cure. The infected fish must be painlessly destroyed and the other fish put in the

DISEASE	SYMPTOMS
ANCHOR WORM	A white worm protrudes from a red, agitated area on the fish's body. Infested fish rubs against anything it can in attempting to scrape off the parasite.
BODY SLIME FUNGUS	The protective slime coating grows white and starts peeling off, as if the fish were shedding or molting. The fins are eventually covered as well.
CHINA DISEASE	Tail fin and other fins begin to fray, beginning at the base of the fin and works its way outward. Affected areas begin to blacken. Ventral region begins to turn black.
CONSTIPATION, INDIGESTION	Fish very inactive, usually rests at the bottom of the tank. More likely than not, its abdomen swells or bulges.
DROPSY (KIDNEY BLOAT)	The belly bloats noticeably and the scales stick out like a pine cone.
FIN CONGESTION	Red blotches, hemorrhages, appear on the trailing edges of the fins. Blood vessels become inflamed and then rupture.
FIN OR TAIL ROT	Fins have missing parts; eventually become shredded. Entire fin will be eaten away.
FISH LICE	Round, disk shaped creatures that clamp onto host and refuse to let go. Infected fish will rub up against objects in the tank in an effort to scrape these pests off.
FISH POX	Whitish or pinkish waxy film develops over the fish's skin and fins.
FUNGUS	Fuzzy growth, different from velvet because it is more whitish and easier to notice.

DISEASE	SYMPTOMS
FURUNCULOSIS	Raised bumps underneath the scales. A short time afterward the bumps rupture and create large bleeding ulcers.
GILL FLUKE	Gills to swell up pink and red and the fish spend lots of time near the surface trying to suck in air. Puss like fluid will be exuded from the gills at this time.
HYDRA	Fry die and are half-eaten or dissolved. Check for cannibalism first among fry.
ICH	Raised white spots about the size of a salt or sugar granule appear on the body and fins.
LEECHES	Long wormlike creatures attached at both ends to fish. Do not come off easily.
MOUTH FUNGUS	White cottony growth on mouth. Sometimes this spreads toward the gills.
POP EYE	Fish's eyes begin to protrude in a very abnormal way.
SKIN FLUKE	Swelled-up coat of some sort. Host fish is constantly trying to rub itself against object to scrape off the infection.
SWIM BLADDER	Fish swim on their sides, upside down, or will somersault as they attempt to swim. Sometimes they can be found either at the bottom or at the top of the tank.
TUMORS	Obvious lumps, bumps, protrusions, sometimes they look like a large blister or wart.
ULCERS	Large red ulcers, boils, dark reddening, and bleeding.
VELVET	Fuzzy area grows with a yellow or golden color.

hospital tank. A ten-day progressive salt treatment isn't a bad idea.

In the meantime, you need to perform an emergency cleaning of the tank. There is no time to waste.

Hydra (not contagious)   This is a small anemonelike freshwater creature. It attaches itself to any stationary objects it can and has small extending stinging tentacles. Hydras are not harmful to adult fish, but these annoying little creatures will have a very happy healthy life living off your fry. Symptoms include half-eaten or dissolved fry. Check for cannibalism first. Maybe you're not feeding your fish enough, or your fry need to be culled.

Since hydras live off live food, fry are a delicious treat for them. If you have hydras, take out the fry and do an emergency cleaning of the tank. Do as much as you can to ensure that none of the old water carrying any these organisms is placed back in the newly sterilized tank.

part four

The
Outdoor
Goldfish

10

Pondkeeping

Goldfish are excellent pond or pool fish. They were originally bred from wild carp and are cold-water freshwater fish. Other than their distant cousin the Koi, goldfish are one of the hardiest and most easily kept pond fish.

There are similarities and differences between keeping an aquarium and keeping a pond. For example, in a pond there is generally not a heater. However, it is important that you read the rest of this book before running out into your backyard and digging a hole for your goldfish.

Where to Place the Pond

This is a tricky proposition for two reasons: Fish need plenty of sunlight and fish need shade. Fish need the sunlight to keep the water relatively warm and to improve and maintain their colors. But if you place too much of the pond in the sun, your pond will be overrun by algae. As we discussed earlier, sunlight makes for a healthy fish. But they need shade, too. Some part of the pond should always be in the shade. Goldfish need a place that will be shaded to cool off from the sun when it gets too hot and goldfish need to be protected from the prying eyes of predators.

Predators are one thing aquarium enthusiasts don't need to worry about. Depending on where you live, there are any number of wild animals that would love a nice fish dinner, including all kinds of birds (including ducks, swans and geese), a few snakes, racoons, weasels, frogs and turtles, and many house pets, especially those cats that don't mind getting wet. If there is a lot of water hyacinths or duckweed for the fish to hide under or escape to, then you will have done well. Also, a fence is not the worst answer to keep out some of these other hungry creatures.

The Pond

Just like a fish tank, your pond should be wider and longer than it is deep. You want as much surface-to-air space as possible. The pond should be no more than, say, three to four feet deep at the deepest part. Just remember, you'll have to be able to pull your fish out too, so don't make the pond too deep, or it will be impossible to get them back.

The pond should be large enough so that sudden temperature changes won't affect the temperature of the water too quickly. Many people have been known to use old large tubs, large children's one-piece plastic pools or strong wood frames hung with layers of heavy-duty plastic sheeting. It just has to be nontoxic and hold water. There are many different shapes and sizes that can be used.

Fantails are good pond fish.

The rule for ponds is thirty square inches of water per one inch of fish. And remember, the larger the space, the faster your goldfish will grow. Within a year to a year and a half, a six-month-old goldfish placed in a pond, if given enough room, will grow to be almost eighteen inches long.

If you are considering breeding in a pond, make sure to leave a shallow end, say, approximately twelve inches deep, for the spawning area. The fish will naturally spawn here, so be sure to have plenty of plant life. This

143

is a good place to feed your fish as well, so that you can
see them clearly and enjoy them more fully.

Three Kinds of Ponds

There are basically three kinds of ponds. The first is
the *molded pond*. These are usually solid single-unit con-
struction and are sold everywhere. The important
thing to know is that the pit that is dug for these ponds
should be lined with about six inches of sand. That
way, as the unit settles as you begin to fill it with water,
there is some play in the earth beneath it so that
the pond can be adjusted slightly before the pond is
filled up.

The *lined pond* has one or more heavy-duty plastic
sheets laid in a deep hole that you have dug in the back
yard. The hole should be at least three to four feet
deep at the deepest end, but should slope to the
ground at all sides. Make sure the bottom has been
smoothed down and that no rocks or anything jagged
pierces the bottom of the pond once it is established,
even if you have to step in it later on.

*A cross section
of a pond.*

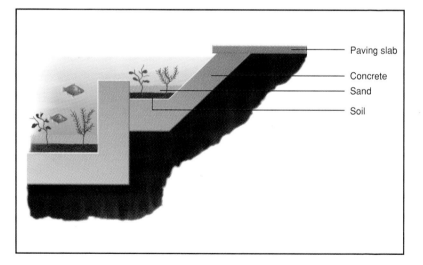

Paving slab

Concrete

Sand

Soil

Again, if you can, spreading a layer of sand on the
bottom is a wonderful idea. The sheet you lay over
the hole should leave an excess of twelve to eighteen

inches on all sides. Water can then be poured in. After the sheet has taken on the shape of the pond, you should lay large rocks or slate slabs on these edges to keep the sheet from moving. The rocks also serve to hide the leftover material.

Some experts like to dig a narrow ditch around the pond, tuck the excess plastic into it with rocks or concrete and then cover them with concrete or slate slabs. Either way, anchor down the sheet.

Then there is the *concrete pond*. If you are ambitious enough to lay a concrete pond, you should make sure that the walls and bottom of the pond are thick and that the concrete used is not porous.

The bottom should be up to twelve inches thick and the walls at least four inches thick. The shape of the pond and what you want to do with it are up to you. Some of the simple shapes, rectangles and squares, for example, can be done by the home do-it-yourselfer.

Much more ambitious ponds can be built by contractors who specialize in such items. Ask your local pet shop owner about this if you are so inclined. Generally, anyone who wants a concrete pond wants one that will last year round. Make sure you have this in mind when choosing a site and size.

> ### SHOULD I HAVE A POND?
>
> This is a question you really should ask your local fish dealer. If you live in a temperate zone, you should be able to keep a pond. If it gets too cold in your area during the winter, where your pond will freeze up and kill the fish, then you should be prepared either to winter your goldfish indoors or to start an aquarium. Ask your local pet dealer for advice as to whether the region you live in is too cold for such an adventure.

Filtering

Goldfish can live in unfiltered ponds. Remember, if your pond is to be unfiltered, make sure that there is plenty of exposed water surface for sufficient aeration to take place. As long as the number of fish is not too great, your pond should be fine. If it is feasible and not too expensive, placing an aerator in an unfiltered pond is an excellent idea. It will keep the water moving and help prevent scum buildup, and it will oxygenate the water. Of course, if you can run an aerator to the pond, you should make an attempt to add a filter.

The best recommendation, of course, is to have a filtered pond. As with all filtering systems, there are two

different kinds of filtering: biological and mechanical. Many are available at your local pet store. Consult with your pet store owner when beginning your pond and let him or her help you pick out a strong and powerful filter. These tend to be larger and more industrial looking than those used by the indoor hobbyist, and they tend to be more expensive, but don't be cheap. Buy a solid filter that will do the job.

The calico Fantail Goldfish is hardy enough to be kept in a pond.

The Fish

As noted in chapter 3, there are numerous fish that can be put in a pond. Here are some of the hardier of the pond breeds. Any metallic or calico colorations will be fine.

- Common Goldfish
- Comet Goldfish
- Black Moor
- Fantail Goldfish
- Pearl-Scale
- Shubunkins
- Wakins

Depending on where you live, the Bubble-eye and the Black Bubble-eye are also considered hardy enough for pond life. Again, the weather must be toward the warmer side and there should be no sharp edges anywhere in the pond.

As with an indoor aquarium, you should make sure that you keep only like fish together. Read Chapter 3 over to make sure of the varieties you plan to foster together. And take size into account as well. Ponds support larger fish. But a twelve-inch goldfish will not tolerate a two-inch inch goldfish for very long. Especially if it's not fed enough.

Plants

For the outdoor goldfish enthusiast, the plants I recommend are water hyacinth and duckweed; crystalwort is also good.

The other plant important in ponds is the water lily. Water lilies don't do well in moving water. They should be packed in a bucket with firm but not hard-packed dirt. Place large gravel on top of the dirt to weigh down the plant. Fill the bucket with water after the lilies have been planted and then place the bucket at the center of the pond. Water lilies are very hardy and can be left out all year as long as there is water in the pond, even if it freezes. Just make sure there are no fish in there if it freezes.

If you want to plant elodea or *Vallisneria* or any other anchored plant, you need to put a few inches of dirt on the entire pond floor. On top of that, you should probably put another couple of inches of sand or large gravel. However, don't use large gravel if you are going to stock the pond with Bubble-eye Goldfish. Make sure to rinse the sand or gravel thoroughly before placing it in the pond.

Feeding

There's good news and there's bad news. The bad news is that you have just supplied the local insects with the best place in the world to breed—a more or less stagnant pond near a house full of humans. Mosquitoes are going to love that! The good news is that your goldfish will love it even more. Those mosquitoes and their larvae will never make it out alive. Many local insects will use your pond for living and breeding purposes. But don't worry, if they do use your pond, your fish will be supplied with an excellent food source and a tasty treat supplied by Mother Nature herself.

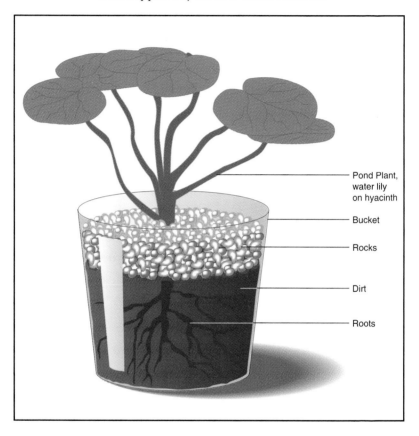

Pond Plant, water lily on hyacinth

Bucket

Rocks

Dirt

Roots

After packing the plants in a bucket, fill it with water and place it in the pond.

The feeding instructions remain the same as for house-kept fish, only more so. In the late summer and autumn you should feed your pond fish three times a day if possible, and you should be feeding them high-carbohydrate foods, as discussed in Chapter 6. It's twice as important to do this for pond fish because they will not feed that much in the winter months—nor should they. The purpose of fattening them up is so that they can winter properly.

In the winter months, if they can, goldfish will root in the mud for warmth and do very little. The cold temperatures will keep them from moving around too much. You should feed them once a day and only enough for five minutes. Don't overfeed them in the winter or in the spring, or you will have fat, lazy goldfish. If winter feeding is done properly, the fish will be heady and active in the spring with thoughts of *l'amour!*

Spawning and Breeding

This is how it's really done on fish farms. It's difficult because it's usually used for group spawning when you have fish all of the same variety. Spawning happens very naturally for pond fish, especially those kept outside year round. They winter naturally and come into spawning season raring to go.

Another reason to have partial shading in a pond is to prevent too much algae. It is thought that too much algae in a pond prevents goldfish from spawning. On the other hand, make sure to have some crystalwort in the pond around this time so that the fish have some around to place their eggs on. Make sure that this is the only place. No matter how much you've made the shallow end a hot bed of spawning, there's always a pair of fish that will use the water hyacinth at the deepest part of the pond.

> ### WATERFALLS
>
> Waterfalls are a place of activity and beauty, and they provide a great source of aeration for a pond. If you have one, the mist forms an excellent environment where plants will be happy to live. As well, the falling water mixes air into the water, providing excellent aeration, and keeps the pond water from developing any stagnation of scum on the water's surface.

If you plan to raise the fry in the pond, remember to extract the adult fish—otherwise the fry will be eaten. Also, if you are raising the fry in the pond, you should be on the lookout for hydra. If there are hydra, remove as many of the fry as you can as soon as possible.

Cleaning

While vacuuming is important in an indoor aquarium, skimming is the best friend an outdoor fish ever had.

Any type of skimmer can be used, so you are better off buying one at a pool equipment store than a pet shop. You need to pull off any large debris and you have to keep the water surface clear. If pond scum builds up, it sometimes ruins aeration.

Algae is also another enemy of the outdoor fish hobbyist. Algae can be a friend in moderation, because it oxygenates the water. However, too much of it can breed too many different bacteria and can eventually foul the water. You need to keep an eye on the algae situation at all times.

The pond needs to be pumped out annually so that you can clean it properly. Follow the instructions for cleaning mentioned in chapter 7. Every couple of months you should attempt a water change of some size—perhaps thirty to seventy-five gallons if you have a large pond and ten or twenty gallons if you have small one. Then use the 10 percent rule every month. Ammonia and other toxins can build up just as a result of normal fish life in a nonfiltered environment. Make sure to use water that has been aged for forty-eight hours.

part five

Beyond the Basics

An Alphabetical Listing of Goldfish

There are over 300 different varieties by body type and coloration in the world. No complete listing exists. A proper classification of goldfish is extremely difficult, since goldfish have been so completely crossbred that it makes any kind of order mainly round about. Here are eighty well-known varieties to give the reader some idea of how many different kinds of goldfish there are in the world. I have placed them in alphabetical order for easier identification purposes.

1. Agard's Wander Goldfish
2. Albino Goldfish
3. American Common Goldfish
4. Barnacled Telescope Goldfish
5. Black Goldfish
6. Black Moor Goldfish
7. Black Lionhead Goldfish
8. Bristol Shubunkin Goldfish
9. Brocaded Goldfish
10. Bubble-eyed Goldfish
11. Calico Common Goldfish
12. Celestial Telescope Goldfish
13. Celestial Veiltail Goldfish
14. Chinese Blue Telescope Goldfish

15. Chinese Marigold Lionhead Goldfish
16. Chinese Tumbler Goldfish
17. Clown Goldfish
18. Colorless Goldfish
19. Comet Goldfish
20. Curled-gill Goldfish
21. Dice or Tumbler Goldfish
22. Dolphin-tailed Goldfish
23. Dolphin-tailed Telescope Goldfish
24. Egg Fish Goldfish
25. European Common Goldfish
26. Fantailed Globe Goldfish
27. Fantailed Goldfish
28. Fantailed Nymph Goldfish
29. Fantailed Pumpkin Goldfish
30. Fringe-tailed Globe Goldfish
31. Fringe-tailed Goldfish
32. Fringe-tailed Nymph Goldfish
33. Fringe-tailed Telescope Goldfish
34. Globe and Tumbler Goldfish
35. Harlequin Goldfish
36. Hog's Nose Comet Goldfish
37. Hog's Nose Goldfish
38. Hooded Globe Goldfish
39. Large or Gorgeous Nymph Goldfish
40. Letter Telescope Goldfish
41. Lionhead Goldfish
42. London Shubunkin Goldfish
43. Mandarin Globe Goldfish
44. Matt Calico Common Goldfish
45. Matt Comet Goldfish
46. Matt Common Goldfish
47. Matt Telescope Goldfish

48. Matt Nymph Goldfish
49. Matt Veiltail Telescope Goldfish
50. Meteor or Tailless Nymph Goldfish
51. Mottled Telescope Goldfish
52. Oranda Goldfish
53. Outfolded Operculum
54. Ovid-eyed Telescope Goldfish
55. Pearl Goldfish
56. Pearl-Scale Goldfish
57. Pompon Goldfish
58. Pompon Oranda Goldfish
59. Pumpkin Goldfish
60. Ram's Nose Comet Goldfish
61. Ram's Nose Goldfish
62. Ranchu Goldfish
63. Ryunkin Goldfish
64. Segmented Sphere-eyed Telescope Goldfish
65. Silver Goldfish
66. Single-tailed Nymph Goldfish
67. Sphere-eyed Telescope Goldfish
68. Swallow-tailed Ryunkin Goldfish
69. Telescope Lionhead Goldfish
70. Tiger Telescope Goldfish
71. Tripod-tailed Goldfish
72. Truncated Cone-eyed Telescope Goldfish
73. Tumbler Telescope Goldfish
74. Twin-tailed Goldfish
75. Veiltail Goldfish
76. Veiltail or Broadtail Ryukin Goldfish
77. Wakin Goldfish
78. Webbed-tailed Goldfish
79. White Rat Goldfish
80. Wild Common Goldfish

Bibliography

Andrew, Dr. Chris. *Fancy Goldfishes.* Morris Plains, N.J.: Tetra Press, 1987.

Axelrod, Dr. Herbert R., and William Vanderwinkler. *Goldfish and Koi in Your Home.* Neptune, N.J.: T.F.H., rev. ed. 1984.

Axelrod, Dr. Herbert R., and Dr. Leonard P. Schultz. *Handbook of Tropical Aquarium Fishes.* Neptune, N.J.: T.F.H., 1990.

Barrie, Anmarie. *Goldfish as a New Pet.* Neptune, N.J.: T.F.H., 1990.

Coborn, John. *Howell Beginner's Guide to Goldfish.* New York: Howell Book House, 1985.

Emmens, Dr. Cliff W. *Tropical Fish: A Complete Introduction.* Neptune, N.J.: T.F.H., 1987.

Geran, James. *The Proper Care of Goldfish.* Neptune, N.J.: T.F.H., 1992.

Goldfish Society of America. *The Official Guide to Goldfish.* Neptune, N.J.: T.F.H., 1991.

Grzimek, Dr. Bernhard, and W. Ladiges. *Grzimek's Animal Life Encyclopedia.* New York: Van Nostrand Reinhold Company, 1973.

Halstead, Bruce W., and Bonnie L. Landa. *Tropical Fish.* New York: Golden Press, 1985.

Hervey, George F., and Jack Hems. *The Goldfish.* London: Faber and Faber, 1968.

Ostrow, Marshall. *Goldfish.* Hauppauge, N.Y.: Barron's, 1985.

Paradise, Paul. *Goldfish.* Neptune, N.J.: T.F.H., 1992.

Penes, B., and I. Tolg. *Goldfish and Ornamental Carp.* Hauppauge, N.Y.: Barron's, 1986.

Piers, Helen. *Taking Care of Your Goldfish.* Hauppauge, N.Y.: Barron's, 1993.

Scheurman, Ines. *Water Plants in the Aquarium.* Hauppauge, N.Y.: Barron's, 1987.

Schnieder, Earl. *All About Aqauriums.* Neptune, N.J.: T.F.H., 1982.

Seto, Zenji. *Goldfish and Fish-Pathology and Its Treatment.* New York: Museum of Natural History Archives, 1934.

Teitler, Neal. *The ABC's of Goldfish.* Neptune, N.J.: T.F.H., 1986.

Wardley Coporation. *Fin Facts Aquarium Handbook.* Secaucus, N.J.: Wardley Corporation, 1992.